Rulers of Ancient Rome

Other Books in the History Makers Series:

Rulers of Ancient Rome

By Don Nardo

Lucent Books
P.O. Box 289011, San Diego, CA 92198-9011

Library of Congress Cataloging-in-Publication Data

Nardo, Don, 1947–
    Rulers of Ancient Rome / by Don Nardo.
        p.   cm. — (History makers)
    Includes bibliographical references and index.
    Summary: Discusses the contributions of various rulers of ancient
Rome, including Fabius, Marius, Caesar, Cicero, Augustus, Nero,
Constantine, and Justinian.
    ISBN 1-56006-356-4 (lib. : alk. paper)
    1. Rome—Biography—Juvenile literature.   2. Heads of state—
Rome—Biography—Juvenile literature.   3. Rome—History—Republic,
265–30 B.C.—Juvenile literature.   4. Rome—History—Empire, 30
B.C.–476 A.D.—Juvenile literature.   [1. Heads of state—Rome.
2. Rome—History—Republic, 265–30 B.C.   3. Rome—History—
Empire. 30 B.C.–476 A.D.   4. Rome—Biography.]   I. Title.   II. Series.
DG203.N37   1999
937'.0099—dc21   98-3841
                                                                               CIP
                                                                               AC

Copyright 1999 by Lucent Books, Inc.
P.O. Box 289011, San Diego, California 92198-9011

Printed in the U.S.A.

CONTENTS

FOREWORD

The literary form most often referred to as "multiple biography" was perfected in the first century A.D. by Plutarch, a perceptive and talented moralist and historian who hailed from the small town of Chaeronea in central Greece. His most famous work, *Parallel Lives*, consists of a long series of biographies of noteworthy ancient Greek and Roman statesmen and military leaders. Frequently, Plutarch compares a famous Greek to a famous Roman, pointing out similarities in personality and achievements. These expertly constructed and very readable tracts provided later historians and others, including playwrights like Shakespeare, with priceless information about prominent ancient personages and also inspired new generations of writers to tackle the multiple biography genre.

The Lucent History Makers series proudly carries on the venerable tradition handed down from Plutarch. Each volume in the series consists of a set of six to eight biographies of important and influential historical figures who were linked together by a common factor. In *Rulers of Ancient Rome*, for example, all the figures were generals, consuls, or emperors of either the Roman Republic or Empire; while the subjects of *Fighters Against American Slavery*, though they lived in different places and times, all shared the same goal, namely the eradication of human servitude. Mindful that politicians and military leaders are not (and never have been) the only people who shape the course of history, the editors of the series have also included representatives from a wide range of endeavors, including scientists, artists, writers, philosophers, religious leaders, and sports figures.

Each book is intended to give a range of figures—some well known, others less known; some who made a great impact on history, others who made only a small impact. For instance, by making Columbus's initial voyage possible, Spain's Queen Isabella I, featured in *Women Leaders of Nations*, helped to open up the New World to exploration and exploitation by the European powers. Unarguably, therefore, she made a major contribution to a series of events that had momentous consequences for the entire world. By contrast, Catherine II, the eighteenth-century Russian queen, and Golda Meir, the modern Israeli prime minister, did not play roles of global impact; however, their policies and actions significantly influenced the historical development of both their own countries and their regional neighbors. Regardless of their relative importance in the greater historical scheme, all of the figures chronicled in the History Makers series made contributions to posterity; and their public achievements, as well as what is known about their private lives, are presented and evaluated in light of the most recent scholarship.

In addition, each volume in the series is documented and substantiated by a wide array of primary and secondary source quotations. The primary source quotes enliven the text by presenting eyewitness views of the times and culture in which each history maker lived; while the secondary source quotes, taken from the works of respected modern scholars, offer expert elaboration and/ or critical commentary. Each quote is footnoted, demonstrating to the reader exactly where biographers find their information. The footnotes also provide the reader with the means of conducting additional research. Finally, to further guide and illuminate readers, each volume in the series features photographs, a chronology, two bibliographies, and a comprehensive index.

The History Makers series provides both students engaged in research and more casual readers with informative, enlightening, and entertaining overviews of individuals from a variety of circumstances, professions, and backgrounds. No doubt all of them, whether loved or hated, benevolent or cruel, constructive or destructive, will remain endlessly fascinating to each new generation seeking to identify the forces that shaped their world.

Many Centuries and Many Hands

The most cursory glance at the march of human history reveals that Roman civilization was extraordinarily long-lived. At least as early as the eighth century B.C., a city-state called Rome existed on the western Italian coast, a tiny kingdom that became a republic in the late sixth century B.C. and over the next several centuries expanded far beyond Italy's borders. Eventually, the republican system became outmoded and unstable; but its collapse did not bring about Rome's end. Instead, the state was transformed into an autocratic empire, a mighty realm that for several more centuries dominated most of the Mediterranean world. Finally, in the late fifth century A.D., that empire disintegrated; yet Rome lived on, for it was only the western part of the realm that had fallen; the eastern part survived for almost another thousand years.

From Revered to Reviled

In these roughly twenty-two centuries of its existence as a national state, Rome underwent numerous political, social, and cultural changes. And not surprisingly, as its governmental system evolved and was modified, it produced leaders of various types, with varying powers, limitations, and goals. Their qualities, both as rulers and human beings, also varied widely. Many were weak or ineffectual and had little or no impact on either their own or later times. By contrast, some were unusually strong, talented, brilliant, ambitious, or vain, and often possessed a mix of these attributes; as a result they became famous, or in some cases infamous, not only in their respective eras, but for all time. Perhaps because they, or at least their reputations, were larger than life, the most revered and reviled rulers are those most often examined in detail in popular histories of Rome.

The lifetimes of the eight leaders examined in this volume occurred during a span of nearly nine hundred years of Roman history, encompassing the periods in which the Roman state, in one

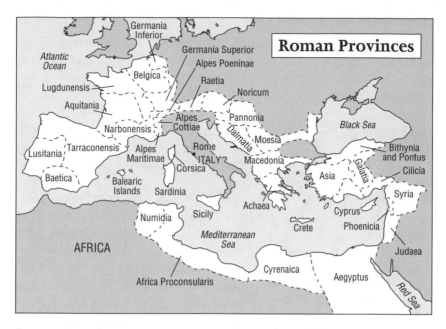

Roman Provinces

form or another, was a major power in the Mediterranean world; each ruler represents a political system or reality and a set of national challenges peculiar to his own time. The first four men were products of republican Rome. Fabius held power during the dark and desperate days of the late second century B.C., when the great Carthaginian general Hannibal invaded Italy and killed more than fifty thousand Romans in a single battle. For engineering the brilliant defensive strategy that ultimately saved the state from destruction, Fabius earned the nickname of "Rome's shield." Marius, who lived a century later, overhauled the Roman army, making it stronger and more professional than ever before; but in doing so he set in motion a process by which army generals could challenge the state for supremacy. A generation later, Caesar, one of the greatest generals of all time, carried that process to its natural limits, making himself dictator for life and bringing the government to its knees. Meanwhile, Cicero, Caesar's chief political nemesis, represented the Senate and republican tradition. Ultimately and tragically submerged in an irresistible tide of civil war and chaos, the stalwart Cicero symbolized the greatness of a Roman system that was passing away.

Rulers of the Empire

The other four men examined were rulers of the new Roman system, the Empire. Augustus, the first and perhaps the greatest emperor, almost single-handedly created the dictatorial imperial government that decided the fate of the Mediterranean world for the next five centuries. Augustus, who died in A.D. 14, showed how autocratic rule could be used in noble, selfless, and constructive ways; Nero, his great-great-grandson and the fifth emperor, exemplified the opposite. Vain and selfish, Nero earned a reputation as one of history's most infamous despots. Constantine, who became emperor in the early fourth century, faced very different problems than either Augustus or Nero had, including serious external threats, in the form of barbarian invaders, and sweeping internal changes, the most prominent stemming from the rise of Christianity. Constantine embraced rather than rejected the new faith, and in so doing transfigured not only Rome but all of Europe for centuries to come. Finally, after the western Empire had fallen to the barbarians, Justinian, who ruled the eastern Empire from its capital, Constantinople, sought to preserve the greatness of Rome's past. His codification of the great body of Roman law profoundly influenced the statecraft and judicial systems of later European societies.

Julius Caesar, whose military brilliance and political ruthlessness facilitated his rise to ultimate power.

Examining the lives and achievements of these eight leaders confirms the truth in the famous adage, "Rome wasn't built in a day." Indeed, Roman civilization, with its many virtues and just as many vices, was the product of many centuries and many hands. Not all of the eight pairs of hands considered here were among the strongest, and many were not the cleanest; but the deeds and works they wrought were definitely among the most memorable.

CHAPTER 1

A Brief History of Ancient Rome

The distant ancestors of Fabius, Caesar, Augustus, and other rulers who would one day lead Rome to power and glory evolved from Latin-speaking tribes that moved from central Europe into Italy perhaps about 2000 B.C.[1] By about the year 1000, the Romans had established primitive villages on seven low hills at a bend in the Tiber River on the edge of the fertile plain of Latium. Stretching for roughly 230 miles southward from the Tiber, the plain is bordered in the west by the Mediterranean Sea and in the east by the rugged Apennines, the mountain range that runs north-south through the Italian boot.

In time, the villages scattered across the Roman hills coalesced into a larger town that became known as Rome. The exact time this happened is unknown; but it is certainly possible that the emergence of the Roman city-state occurred within a century or so of 753 B.C., the year, as calculated by later Roman scholars, that Romulus, the first important Roman ruler, founded the city.[2] According to the most popular of the several founding legends, after the Greeks sacked the city of

Romulus, the legendary founder of Rome, may actually have been one of the city's early kings.

Troy, in Asia Minor (what is now Turkey), circa 1200 B.C., the Trojan prince Aeneas escaped and sailed westward to Italy. There, in Latium, he married an Italian princess and from their union sprang a line of noble rulers leading to Romulus. The great first-century B.C. Roman historian Livy tells how, by killing his brother Remus,

> Romulus obtained the sole power. . . . [His] first act was to fortify the Palatine, the scene of his own upbringing. He

offered sacrifice to the gods. . . . Having performed with proper ceremony his religious duties, he summoned his subjects and gave them laws. . . . Meanwhile Rome was growing. . . . To help fill his big new town, [Romulus] threw open . . . a place of asylum for fugitives. Hither fled for refuge all the [outcasts] from the neighboring peoples; some free, some slaves, and all of them wanting nothing more than a fresh start.[3]

Romulus's welcoming of foreigners into the city, like the non-Italian origins of Aeneas, were among attempts by later Romans to explain the cosmopolitan nature of their state. As noted scholar T. J. Cornell explains:

The Roman foundation legend provides evidence, first and foremost, of how the Romans of later times chose to see themselves. . . . The most revealing sign of this is the way it defines the identity of the Roman people as a mixture of different ethnic groups, and of Roman culture as the product of various foreign influences. . . . The Roman saga was characteristic of a people who had built up their power by extending their citizenship and continuously admitting new elements into their midst.[4]

A Genius for the Political

Besides a willingness to absorb new peoples and ideas, another of Rome's strengths was an innate genius for political organization and rule. After a period of domination by kings, in about 509 B.C. the state's leading citizens, the patricians, all well-to-do landholders, provided the first major demonstration of this genius. Boldly expelling their king, Tarquinius Superbus, they established the Roman Republic, a new government run, at least in theory, by representatives of the people.

However, Roman leaders at first defined "the people" rather narrowly. Only free adult males who owned weapons (and were therefore eligible for military service), a minority of the population, could vote or hold public office. Some of these citizens met periodically in a body called the Assembly, which proposed and voted on new laws and also annually elected two consuls, or administrator-generals, to run the state and lead the army. The other legislative body, the Senate, was composed exclusively of patricians, who held their positions for life. Because the senators usually dictated the policies of the consuls and, through the use of wealth and high position, indirectly influenced the way

A Roman bas-relief depicts a group of senators on their way to a session. During Rome's republican centuries, the Senate was the government's most powerful legislative body.

the members of the Assembly voted, the Senate held the real power in Rome.

Yet though most Romans did not have a say in state policy, many had a measurable voice in choosing leaders and making laws. And these laws often offered an umbrella of protection for members of all classes against the arbitrary abuses of potentially corrupt leaders. "Law is the bond which assures to each of us his honorable life within our commonwealth [empire]," Cicero wrote in the first century B.C., "the foundation of liberty, the fountainhead [main source] of justice. It is what keeps the heart and mind . . . and feeling of our nation alive."[5] For these and other reasons, republican government proved increasingly flexible and largely met the needs of Romans of all classes.

As a result, the people came to view their system with intense pride and patriotism and to feel that the gods favored Rome above all other cities. Such feelings of superiority soon fueled the first stages of Roman expansion. In the fifth century B.C., Roman armies began marching outward from Latium and subduing neighboring peoples, including the Samnites, a powerful hill tribe of south-central Italy. Instead of ruling such conquered peoples with an iron fist, the Romans introduced to them the Latin language, as well as Roman ideas, laws, and customs.[6] In addition to this "Romanization" process, Rome forged long-lasting alliances with many of its former enemies. "What made the Romans so remarkable," comments the prolific classical scholar Michael Grant, was a talent for patient political reasonableness that was unique in the ancient world. . . . On the whole, Rome found it advisable . . . to keep its bargains with its allies, displaying a self-restraint, a readiness to compromise, and a calculated generosity that the world had never seen. And so the allies, too, had little temptation to feel misused. . . . After the end of the Samnite wars [about 290 B.C.] a network of such agreements was extended across the whole of central Italy.[7]

Extraordinary Spirit and Audacity

Almost immediately after the Samnite wars, the Romans turned on the numerous Greek cities that had sprung up across southern Italy in the preceding few centuries. Some of these cities were larger and all were more culturally advanced and splendid than Rome, which was still a relatively small, dirty, and uncultured community. But the Italian Greeks were disunited and their armies could not match the size and caliber of those fielded by Rome. By 265 B.C., the Romans had absorbed the Greek lands and become the undisputed masters of all Italy south of the Po Valley, the fertile northern region lying at the foot of the Alps.

Rome next cast its gaze beyond the shores of Italy and onto the other coasts of the sea's western sphere, a region then largely controlled by Carthage, a powerful trading city located at the northern tip of Tunisia, on the African coast. From 264 to 241, Rome and Carthage grappled in the most devastating war fought anywhere in the world up to that time. Rome won this so-called First Punic War in large degree because it took the bold step of creating its very first fleet of warships.[8] This was a classic demonstration of the Romans' renowned practicality, resourcefulness, and determination. According to the second-century B.C. Greek historian Polybius, they built some 120 warships in only sixty days:

> They faced great difficulties because their shipwrights were completely inexperienced in the building of [large warships]. . . . Yet it is this fact which illustrates better than any other the extraordinary spirit and audacity of the Romans' decision. It was not a question of having adequate resources for the enterprise, for they had in fact none whatsoever. . . . But once they had conceived the idea, they embarked on it so boldly, that without waiting to gain any experience in naval warfare they immediately engaged the Carthaginians, who had for generations enjoyed an unchallenged supremacy at sea.[9]

14

Rome went on to fight and win two more bloody wars with Carthage. The Second Punic War (218–202) involved a devastating assault on Italy by Carthage's brilliant war leader Hannibal; greatly aided by the leadership of Fabius, the Romans managed eventually to defeat the invaders, but only at a terrible cost—the loss of nearly an entire generation of Roman men. In the brief but horrendously violent Third Punic War (149–147), the Romans exacted final vengeance against their archenemy by invading Africa and quite literally erasing the once mighty Carthage from the map.

Next, Rome turned eastward and attacked the Greek kingdoms clustered in the sea's eastern sphere. The first of these states to fall to Roman steel was Macedonia, consisting mainly of Greece and parts of Asia Minor; not long afterward, Rome defeated the Seleucid kingdom, centered in the Near East; and finally, in 167, the Ptolemaic kingdom, made up largely of Egypt, wisely submitted to Rome without a fight. After a century of unparalleled military successes, the Mediterranean Sea had become, in effect, a Roman lake. Indeed, the Romans came, rather arrogantly, to call it *mare nostrum*, "our sea."

The Failure of the Senate

Rome had been so successful, in fact, that as the second century B.C. drew to a close no one then living could have predicted the political and social chaos, almost continuous civil strife, and horrific death toll the Republic would experience in the next seven decades. The causes of these troubles were various. In their recent

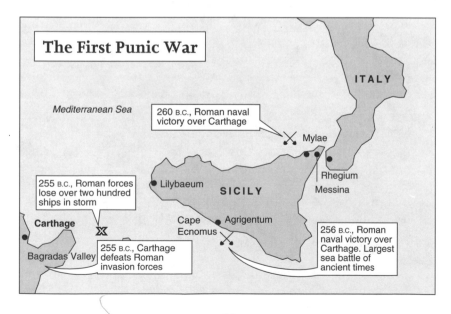

The First Punic War

Mediterranean Sea

ITALY

260 B.C., Roman naval victory over Carthage

Mylae

Rhegium

255 B.C., Roman forces lose over two hundred ships in storm

Lilybaeum

SICILY

Messina

Carthage

Cape Ecnomus

Agrigentum

256 B.C., Roman naval victory over Carthage. Largest sea battle of ancient times

Bagradas Valley

255 B.C., Carthage defeats Roman invasion forces

conquests the Romans had amassed tremendous political and military power and influence throughout most of the known world, as well as great wealth. But they now began to find that administering such large and far-flung territories was no easy task. Their political system, originally designed to rule a single city-state inhabited by one people, did not work nearly as well on the scale of a vast collection of nations composed of many diverse peoples. As a result, Rome encountered an increasingly difficult struggle to maintain order in its empire.

Rome's conquest of most of the lands bordering the Mediterranean Sea in its republican years was made possible by its well-trained and highly disciplined soldiers, some of whom are portrayed in this carved relief.

The struggle for order also became internal, as military strongmen vied for control of the state itself. In centuries past, of course, the Senate had largely run the show in Rome. The consuls and other generals and public officials had given their allegiance to the state, as had the armies themselves. But by the beginning of the fateful first century B.C., the army had evolved from a militia made up mostly of landowners into a more professional force composed of volunteers from all classes. These largely poorer, less educated soldiers, comments historian F. R. Cowell, were more "excitable and unsteady, [and] ready to back almost any man who would offer them land and bread. They were therefore a standing invitation to political adventurers." [10]

Marius was the first of a new breed of military strongmen who amassed such personal armies. Many others, including his famous nephew, Julius Caesar, followed. These generals took advantage of the fact that the Roman government had not seen fit to provide pensions of land or money for retiring troops. In this and other similar ways, the Senate, mired in tradition and slow to adapt to new political realities, had failed; and the price it paid was collapse, both of its own authority and of the government of which it was the primary guiding force. "The Republic was finished," stated the late, great classical historian A. H. M. Jones:

> The old habit whereby magistrates . . . obeyed [the Senate's] instructions no longer prevailed. Armies obeyed the orders of their commanders, even to fight the government of Rome. . . . A possible remedy might have been to have gone back to the pre-Marian army, and conscript unwilling freeholders, who would not have supported their commanders in civil wars. Another remedy might have been for the state to supply land allotments for discharged soldiers, who would not wish to jeopardize them by rebellion. Neither remedy was suggested. [11]

Rome at Its Zenith

The government's authority having eroded, for three generations devastating civil wars wracked the Mediterranean world, killing hundreds of thousands of people and leaving the survivors fearful and war-weary. From this seemingly relentless strife, one man finally emerged victorious—Octavian, Caesar's adopted son. After defeating his last rivals, the Roman general Mark Antony and Egypt's Queen Cleopatra, in a huge naval battle near Actium (in western Greece) in 31 B.C., Octavian, renamed Augustus, "the exalted one," began building a new, more autocratic Roman state on the wreckage of the now defunct Republic. Though he never personally used the title of emperor, he was in fact the first ruler of the realm that became known as the Roman Empire.

Augustus and most of his immediate successors were thoughtful, effective rulers who brought peace and economic stability to

the Roman world. The two major exceptions were the unbalanced Caligula (reigned A.D. 37–41), the first emperor to be assassinated, and the self-centered Nero (54–68), the first to be declared an enemy of the people. However, their reigns, though in many ways corrupt and/or ineffective, did no measurable harm to the Empire's overall prosperity; consequently, the highly productive period lasting from about 30 B.C. to A.D. 180 became known as the *Pax Romana*, or "Roman Peace."

The five emperors who ruled from 96 to 180—Nerva, Trajan, Hadrian, Antoninus Pius, and Marcus Aurelius—were particularly capable and enlightened (hence the nickname later accorded them, the "five good emperors"). They brought Roman civilization to its political, economic, and cultural zenith, prompting the famous eighteenth-century English historian Edward Gibbon to remark:

This famous statue of Augustus Caesar, found at Prima Porta, near Rome, was carved during his fruitful forty-five-year reign by an unknown sculptor.

> If a man were called upon to fix the period in the history of the world during which the condition of the human race was most happy and prosperous, he would without hesitation name that which elapsed from the accession of Nerva to the death of Aurelius. . . . Their united reigns are possibly the only period of history in which the happiness of a great people was the sole object of government.[12]

Under Trajan, the Empire was larger than it ever had been or would be. It stretched from the Atlantic Ocean in the west to the Persian Gulf in the east, and from northern Africa in the south to central Britain in the north, a colossal political unit encompassing some 3.5 million square miles and some 100 million people.

A Crisis of Epic Proportions

Unfortunately for Rome, the passing of Marcus Aurelius in 180 marked the end of the prosperous and largely happy *Pax Romana*. Thereafter, the Empire's political and economic problems rapidly increased, leading to a century of severe crisis in which the Roman realm approached the brink of total collapse. The crisis had several dimensions and causes, first among them poor leadership. In contrast to the honest and able rulers of the second century, most of those who followed were ambitious, brutal, and/or incompetent individuals who had little or no concept of how to deal with the serious problems the Empire now faced.

Perhaps chief among these problems was the economy, which steadily worsened. By the end of the second century, most of Rome's gold and silver mines had been depleted. The lack of precious metals forced the government to mint coins containing cheaper alloys, which, because money was worth less, led to rising inflation. The economy also suffered because of declining agriculture. More and more small farmers, unable to compete with large farming estates known as *latifundia*, owned by wealthy individuals or the state, abandoned their fields. The out-of-work farmers became part of the growing class of agrarian poor. Some migrated to

The emperor Trajan, one of the so-called "good emperors," stands (second from right) with important members of his court.

19

the cities and lived on free bread distributed by the government; others remained on the land and became *coloni*, low-paid tenant workers on the larger farms. Desperate, they became financially dependent on their employers, who often took advantage of legal procedures to bind them and their descendants to the same jobs for generations. According to historian Arthur Boak, although "they were not absolutely under the power of the owner and could not be disposed of [sold] by him apart from the land . . . as time went on their condition tended to approximate more and more to servitude. 'Slaves of the soil,' they were called."[13]

The emperors of the late second century and much of the third century also faced grave military threats and problems. Large seminomadic Germanic tribes posed formidable threats to the Empire's northern borders during the reign of Marcus Aurelius and these threats continued and worsened under his successors. Moreover, the Roman army charged with meeting these threats, its ranks increasingly filled with noncitizens from northern border areas, was less disciplined and reliable than it had been in the past.

This intricate relief depicts Marcus Aurelius, last of the "good emperors," parading in his chariot, while a trumpeter (right, rear) blows a fanfare.

Eventually, the Empire faced a crisis of epic proportions. By the early 230s, money was nearly worthless and poverty and crime were widespread. Compounding these and other domestic problems, hordes of Germans poured into the provinces of Gaul, what is now France and Belgium. Unable to deal with so many internal and external threats simultaneously, Rome's military and administrative structure buckled. The result was a period of near anarchy, some fifty years of chaos and civil war that almost destroyed the Empire. Repeatedly, army units in various parts of the realm swore allegiance to their generals, who then tried to fight one another while defending against invaders, a foolhardy endeavor. Between 235 and 284, more than fifty rulers claimed the throne, only half of whom were legally recognized, and all but one died by assassination or other violent means.

As they attack a German fortress, Roman soldiers raise their shields in a testudo, *or "turtle," formation to protect against arrows, rocks, and other missiles.*

Diocletian's Reforms

Disunity, chaos, and enemy incursions appeared to spell the end of the old Roman world. However, beginning in the year 268, a series of strong military leaders took control and in one of the most remarkable reversals in history the stubborn and resilient Romans managed to regain the initiative. In the span of about sixteen years, these rulers managed to push back the Germans and also to defeat illegal imperial claimants in various parts of the realm.

With the Empire reunited and minimal order restored, in 284 a remarkably intelligent and capable man assumed the throne. He was Diocletian, who, like Augustus three centuries before, took on the task of completely reorganizing the Roman state after a period of serious disorders. Among the first of his sweeping reforms was the transformation of the imperial government and court into an "eastern"-style monarchy similar to those in Egypt and Persia, where the ruler was addressed as "Lord" and people bowed deeply when approaching him. Diocletian also drastically overhauled the Roman economy. To make sure that goods and services continued uninterrupted, he ordered that nearly all workers remain in their present professions for life. In addition, he attempted

21

to regulate prices and wages, believing that such an effort would keep inflation down and the economy moving smoothly.[14]

Perhaps Diocletian's most important reform was the reorganization of the Empire itself. Realizing that administering so vast a realm was too difficult for one man, he divided the Empire in half. He himself took charge of the eastern sector, ruling from the city of Nicomedia in northern Asia Minor, and he appointed a general named Maximian as ruler of the western sector. In 293, Diocletian further divided imperial power. He and Maximian each retained the title of Augustus and appointed an assistant emperor with the title of Caesar, creating a four-man combination often referred to as the Tetrarchy. Another administrative reform overhauled the provincial bureaucracy. "Military and civil commands were separated," explains scholar Averil Cameron,

> and each province henceforth had both a military commander [the *dux*, or duke] and a civil governor. The provinces themselves were reduced in size and greatly enlarged in number [from about fifty to one hundred]. . . . The aim was to secure greater efficiency by shortening the chain of communications and command, and in so doing to reduce the power of individual governors.[15]

The Decline of the West

Another hallmark of Diocletian's reign was that he was the last emperor to stage a large-scale persecution of the Christians, an unpopular religious sect whose members constituted somewhere between 2 and 10 percent of the Empire's population by the year 300. At this time many Romans still held the misconception that the Christians were dangerous fanatics who hated all humanity and wanted to destroy the established order. However, despite frequent persecutions, the Christians persevered and their ranks continued to grow. Their biggest early boost came from Constantine (reigned 307–337), who guaranteed them absolute toleration and provided for the restoration of all of the property they had lost in the persecutions.

Another of Constantine's achievements that had major and lasting effects on the Empire was his establishment of a new Roman capital in the realm's eastern sector. Constantinople, the "City of Constantine," was formally inaugurated on May 11, 330, marking the beginning of what would become a permanent division of the Roman world into western and eastern spheres. Over time these spheres grew increasingly distant and distinct from each other, and the split became more or less unalterable in 395 when

Theodosius, the last emperor to rule over both east and west, died. From this time on, there were two Roman governments, two royal courts, and increasingly two national policies.

Meanwhile, in the final decades of the fourth century the pressure of the barbarian tribes on the northern borders was increasing. In 375, the Huns, a fierce nomadic people from central Asia, swept into eastern Europe, driving the Goths and other Germanic peoples into the Roman border provinces; and the Roman army, now not nearly as strong, disciplined, and mobile as it had been in the Empire's heyday, was increasingly unsuccessful in stopping the

These fifth-century ivory plaques symbolize the Empire's old and new capitals, Rome (left) (in which the figure wears a military helmet), and Constantinople (the crown bearing a likeness of the city's walls).

invaders. The province of Britain had to be abandoned in about 407 and in the succeeding decades various tribal peoples settled permanently in other western provinces.

Perhaps the biggest single shock to the Empire came in 410, when Alaric, king of the Visigoths (or "Wise Goths"), besieged and captured Rome. The Christian writer Jerome cried out, "My voice is choked with sobs as I dictate these words. The city that has conquered the universe is now herself conquered. . . . She dies of hunger before dying by the sword." [16] This was an exaggeration, for Rome was still very much intact. The invaders had plundered much gold and other valuables, but had stayed only three days and destroyed few buildings. The situation was worse, however, when Rome was sacked a second time in 455, this time by the Vandals, who plundered the city for fourteen days before departing.

The western Empire had by now shrunk to a pale ghost of the mighty state of the *Pax Romana*. The last few western emperors ruled over a pitiful realm consisting only of the Italian peninsula and portions of a few nearby provinces; even these lands were not safe or secure, for claims on Roman territory continued. In 476, a German-born general named Odoacer, who commanded the last of all Roman armies in Italy, demanded that he and his soldiers be granted lands in which to settle. When the government refused, Odoacer's men acclaimed him as king of Italy and, on September 4, deposed the young emperor Romulus Augustulus. No new em-

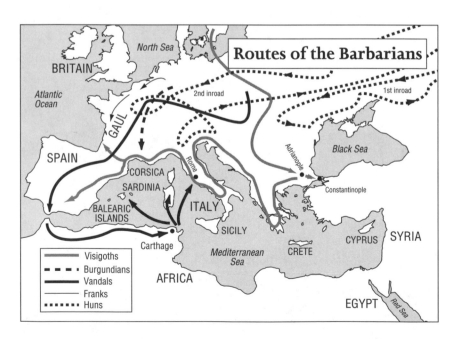

peror took the boy's place and most later scholars came to view the event as the fall of the western Empire.

Political Decline, Cultural Survival

In the half century or so following 476, Italy and what was left of the western provinces were governed by barbarian kings. The eastern emperor Justin I (reigned 518–527) later tentatively recognized the legitimacy of one of these kings, Theodoric the Ostrogoth; but Justin did so mainly because he lacked the will to organize the massive army and resources needed to take back the western sphere by force. The situation changed when Justin's more ambitious nephew, Justinian I (reigned 527–565) succeeded him. In 533, Justinian's capable general Belisarius wrested northern Africa from the Vandals and then proceeded to attack the Goths in Italy, which was largely regained by about 555.

Over time, however, these prodigious efforts came to nothing. In 568, another tribal people, the Lombards, descended into and captured northern and central Italy; and in the following century Muslim armies swept through northern Africa, ending Constantinople's influence there. After that, eastern Rome, in the form of the Byzantine Empire, controlled mainly parts of Greece and Asia Minor, a realm that grew progressively smaller and weaker until Constantinople itself fell to the Ottoman Turks in 1453. As it turned out, Justinian's codification of all existing Roman laws, like many other aspects of Roman culture that survived the ages, proved to have a far stronger influence on Western societies than any kind of political or military authority. As scholar Solomon Katz points out, "In the long perspective of history, the survival of Roman civilization, [in the form of the cultural] heritage which generation after generation has accepted, is perhaps more significant than the decline of Rome." [17]

CHAPTER 2

Fabius: Shield of the Roman People

Quintus Fabius Maximus, whom Romans long remembered as a war hero, a leader of vision, resolve, and honor, and a savior of the state, came from one of the oldest and most distinguished patrician families. The Fabii claimed descent from the legendary semidivine adventurer Hercules. Sometime in the dim past, the story went, Hercules visited Italy and made love to a local woman, who gave birth to the founder of the clan. One of the most celebrated of the early Fabii, Fabius's grandfather, surnamed Rullus, was elected consul five times and in 295 B.C. led an army to victory over a coalition of Samnites and other Italian peoples. For these achievements, Rullus came to be called Maximus, meaning "greatest," a name that his illustrious grandson, born about 275, would also bear.

According to the renowned first-century A.D. Greek biographer Plutarch, the young Fabius bore two affectionate nicknames. One was Verrucosus (meaning "wart-covered"), because of a small but prominent wart on his upper lip.[18] The other was Ovicula ("little lamb"), because of his quiet and gentle manner. He "showed an extraordinary caution even when he was indulging in childhood pleasures," writes Plutarch,

> and learned his lessons slowly and laboriously; and these characteristics, combined with his docile, almost submissive behavior towards his companions, led those who did not know him thoroughly to suppose that he was dull and stupid. It was only a few who could see beyond these superficial qualities and discern the greatness of spirit . . . and the unshakable resolution which lay in the depths of his soul. . . . He soon proved to all alike that his apparent lack of energy was really due to his . . . soundly based judgment, while the fact that he never acted on impulse . . . meant that he was steadfast and resolute in all circumstances.[19]

This drawing shows Fabius (on horse), shortly after becoming dictator, accompanied by twenty-four attendants known as lictors, *who carry fasces, symbols of Roman power.*

In time, Fabius's qualities of good judgment and unshakable resolution would save thousands of Roman lives and win him the eternal gratitude of his countrymen.

"We Give You War"

Almost nothing is known of Fabius's early career. His first recorded political distinction was his election in 233 B.C. to the consulship, the first of five times he would be so honored. That year also witnessed his first noteworthy military exploit, the defeat of the Ligurians, the inhabitants of the coastal region of extreme northwestern Italy, who had been raiding nearby Roman settlements.

The chain of events that led to Fabius's most impressive and famous deeds did not begin until 218, when he was almost sixty years old. This was the year in which the second war against Carthage erupted, a long and devastating conflict that would send hundreds of thousands of people from both sides to untimely graves. After its defeat by Rome at the end of the First Punic War (241), Carthage, led at first by its strong general Hamilcar Barca, invaded Spain. The Carthaginians gained more and more territory

Hannibal leads his army through treacherous Alpine passes on the journey toward northern Italy. Scholars still debate the exact route the Carthaginians took.

there, eventually causing concern in Rome. In an effort to ensure that Carthage would not extend its influence any farther into Europe, circa 226 the Romans made an alliance with Saguntum, a city-state on Spain's eastern coast; this association, Rome hoped, would create a barrier to further Carthaginian expansion.

But the Roman plan failed. In 221, the ambitious and talented Hannibal, Hamilcar's son, inherited command of Carthaginian Spain. In the following year, Hannibal boldly attacked and laid siege to Saguntum, eventually taking the city at the cost of the lives of most of its inhabitants.[20] Hearing of Saguntum's demise, the indignant Romans sent ambassadors, among their number the noble Fabius, directly to Carthage. Their message was straight to the point—surrender Hannibal or face a new war with Rome. When the Carthaginian senate refused, writes Livy, Fabius

> laid his hand on the fold of his toga, where he had gathered it at the breasts, and "Here," he said, "we bring you peace and war. Take which you will." Scarcely had he spoken, when the answer no less proudly rang out: "Whichever you please—we do not care." Fabius let the gathered folds fall, and cried: "We give you war." The

Carthaginian senators replied, as one man: "We accept it; and in the same spirit we will fight it to the end."[21]

War having been declared, most Roman leaders assumed they could attain victory fairly quickly and easily. But they had not reckoned on the daring, fortitude, and genius of their main opponent, Hannibal. He decided on a bold strategy for which the Romans were totally unprepared. They knew he had no war fleets, so he could not sail from Spain to Italy to attack Rome; and if he tried a landward approach, he would come up against the towering, snow-covered Alps, which the Romans viewed as a barrier no army could cross. From their perspective, therefore, Italy was safe. In one of the cleverest and most audacious military moves ever executed, however, Hannibal surprised the Romans by crossing the Alps in the spring of 218.

A Cautious and Shrewd Policy

When Hannibal suddenly appeared in the Po Valley with some twenty thousand infantry and six thousand cavalry, the two consuls, Publius Cornelius Scipio and Tiberius Sempronius Longus, frantically gathered their forces and pitted them against his advance. But their efforts were in vain. In the following months Hannibal delivered the Romans three serious defeats, the first two on the Ticinus and Trebia, tributaries of the Po River; and the

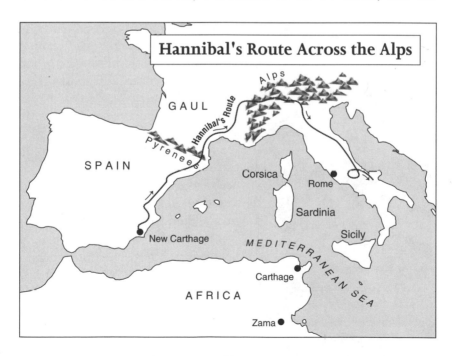

Hannibal's Route Across the Alps

third at Lake Trasimene, only seventy miles north of Rome. In the last encounter, in which fifteen thousand Roman soldiers died, the sounds of slaughter were so deafening that no one detected another momentous event happening simultaneously. "At the critical moment in the action," Plutarch recalls,

> an earthquake took place which destroyed several cities, diverted rivers from their channels, and split off great fragments of cliffs, and yet in spite of the violence of the catastrophe, none of those who were engaged in the battle noticed it all.[22]

Hannibal, whose losses in these engagements had been minimal, was now in a strategic position to strike at Rome's capital

Hannibal, Carthage's greatest general, watches solemnly as his troops prepare for their fateful trek over the Alps.

city. In this dire emergency, the Romans activated a rarely used constitutional provision that allowed for the appointment of a "dictator," an individual holding almost total authority over the nation. A dictator was expected to use his sweeping powers to fend off impending disaster and then to step down after serving for six months. Because of his reputation for honesty and sound judgment, Fabius was chosen as dictator in the late spring of 217 B.C. He immediately set in motion new recruiting programs to replenish Rome's crippled army ranks; at the same time he destroyed the bridges leading to Rome and burned all the crops in the vicinity to deny Hannibal the use of these valuable resources.

However, to the Romans' surprise, Hannibal did not attack the capital. Instead, he swerved around Rome and moved into south-central Italy, there hoping to incite rebellions among the Samnites and other peoples the Romans had conquered in the preceding century. Without their support, he reasoned, Rome's power base would collapse. As for Fabius, he was far less worried about Italian defections to Hannibal than about losing any more able-bodied troops, at that moment the country's most precious resource. So the newly appointed dictator instituted a cautious and very shrewd policy in dealing with Hannibal. Plutarch explains:

> [Fabius] was determined not to fight a pitched battle, and since he had time and manpower . . . on his side, his plan was to exhaust his opponent's strength . . . by means of delaying tactics, and gradually to wear down his small army and meager resources. With this object in view he always camped in mountainous country, where he was out of the reach of the enemy's cavalry, and at the same time hung menacingly over the Carthaginian camp. If the enemy stayed still, he did the same. If they moved, he would make a detour, descend a little distance from the heights, and show himself just far enough away to prevent himself from being forced into action against his will, but near enough to create the suspicion . . . that he might be about to attack.[23]

Fabius Afraid to Fight?

Although Fabius's tactics, which earned him the nickname Cunctator, "the Delayer" (and which have been called Fabian ever since), were effective, they were increasingly unpopular among his own people. Often, Hannibal's soldiers ravaged farms and villages in plain sight of Roman troops, who were forbidden by the dictator from interfering. Many Romans, especially military men, became convinced that Fabius was refusing to engage the enemy because he was afraid to fight.

According to Livy, Hannibal learned of the growing Roman discontent with his opponent and cleverly succeeded in adding to it. Finding out the location of Fabius's country estate, the Carthaginian leader ordered "that no damage of any kind . . . was to be done to it, though everything else in the neighborhood was to be utterly destroyed."[24] Hannibal's intention, of course, was to suggest to the Romans that he and Fabius had a secret pact and that the estate had been spared as payment for the dictator's nonaggressive tactics.

Fabius eventually became so unpopular that his own second in command, Marcus Minucius Rufus, loudly lectured and insulted him in front of the soldiers. "Are we here," cried Minucius,

> merely to enjoy the pleasant spectacle of our friends being butchered and their houses burned? Are we not ashamed, if

for nothing else, at least for these citizens of ours? . . . To imagine a war can be won by doing nothing whatever . . . is folly: soldiers must be armed; they must be led into the field of battle; you must meet your enemy man against man. Rome's power grew by action and daring—not by these do-nothing tactics, which the faint-hearted call caution.[25]

Minucius later spoke words to the same effect to the Roman Assembly. Though its members lacked the courage to compel the dictator to step down, they did grant Minucius authority equal to Fabius's, an unprecedented act in Roman politics. Setting out with an army, the impetuous Minucius soon found and attacked some of Hannibal's forces. It did not take long for the Carthaginians to get the upper hand and Minucius and his men would surely have been wiped out if it had not been for Fabius, who suddenly appeared with his own soldiers and forced the enemy to retreat. Impressed by Fabius's display of valor, the wily Hannibal is reported to have quipped, "Haven't I kept telling you that the cloud we have seen hovering over the mountain tops would burst one day like a tornado?"[26]

Catastrophe at Cannae

After the battle, everyone expected Fabius to seek out Minucius and berate and punish him for his poor judgment; but the mild-mannered and forgiving Fabius retired to his tent without uttering a word. Instead, it was Minucius, humbled by the experience, who sought out Fabius and said:

> Dictator, on this day you have won two victories, one over Hannibal through your bravery, and the other over your colleague through your generalship and your generosity. With the first you have saved our lives, and with the second you taught us a lesson. . . . I call you by the name of Father, because it is the most honorable that I can use. . . . My father gave me life, but you have saved not only this but the lives of all the men under me.[27]

Unfortunately for Rome, other leaders did not profit by the lesson Fabius had taught Minucius. When Fabius dutifully laid down his six-month appointment at the end of 217 B.C., hotter heads vied for power in the consular elections for the following year. With the blessings of most of the senators, the new consuls, Gaius Terentius Varro and Lucius Aemilius Paullus, reversed Fabius's policy in dealing with Hannibal. At the head of a new army, perhaps seventy thousand strong, Varro and Paullus advanced on the enemy, who was then camped at Cannae, a southern Italian town near the Adriatic coast. With forces numbering forty-five thousand at most, Hannibal was clearly outnumbered.[28] Yet when the two armies met on August 2, 216, this tactical genius engineered one of the most stunning and complete victories in military history. According to Polybius's account:

> The fighting which developed was truly barbaric. . . . The [end] result was exactly what Hannibal had planned: [most of] the Romans . . . were trapped. . . . As their outer

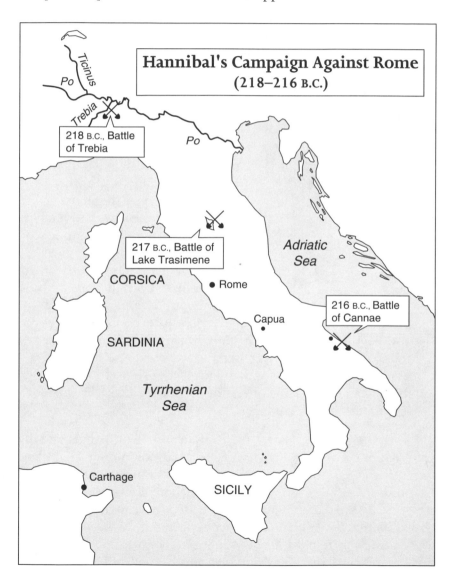

Hannibal's Campaign Against Rome
(218–216 B.C.)

218 B.C., Battle of Trebia

217 B.C., Battle of Lake Trasimene

216 B.C., Battle of Cannae

Adriatic Sea

CORSICA

Rome

Capua

SARDINIA

Tyrrhenian Sea

Carthage

SICILY

Po

Ticinus

Trebia

Po

ranks were continually cut down and the survivors were forced to pull back and huddle together, they were finally all killed where they stood.[29]

The catastrophe at Cannae was the worst single military defeat in Rome's long history. Over fifty thousand Romans were slain, including the consul Paullus and some eighty senators; by contrast, Hannibal lost only six thousand men.

The Spirit of the State, the Father of the People

Rome had learned the hard way that Fabius's attempt to wear Hannibal down while sparing Roman lives had been the wiser approach. And it was he who now held the people together in their moment of darkest despair. "It was upon Fabius that the Romans centered their last hopes," writes Plutarch:

Hannibal (247–183 B.C.), in a likeness taken from a coin. In time, he came to fear and respect Fabius Maximus.

His wisdom was the sanctuary to which men fled for refuge . . . and they believed that it was his practical capacity above all which had preserved the unity of Rome at this moment, and had prevented her citizens from deserting the city. . . . For when the people had felt secure, it was Fabius who had appeared to be cautious and timid, but now, when all others were giving way to boundless grief and helpless bewilderment, he was the only man to walk the streets with a resolute step, a serene expression, and a kindly voice. . . . [He] made himself the strength and the moving spirit of all the offices of the state, since every man looked to him for guidance.[30]

In the years that followed, the Romans relied on Fabius and his proven policy of delaying, harassing, and containing Hannibal. Fabius and another highly respected commander, Marcus Claudius Marcellus, soon worked out an effective alternating strategy. Fabius continuously frustrated and wore down the enemy, while, when Hannibal least expected it, Marcellus periodically struck at him with bold, lightninglike attacks. Seeing that this combination of Fabius's caution and Marcellus's audacity was successful, the people often reelected the pair as consuls. They came to call Fabius Rome's mighty shield and Marcellus its trusty sword; and indeed, Hannibal himself declared that he feared and respected Fabius for keeping him from inflicting losses on the Romans, and Marcellus for his ability to inflict losses on him. The new strategy succeeded in neutralizing Hannibal, who eventually realized the futility of trying to conquer Italy. In 203 B.C. he returned to Africa and the following year suffered his first and only major defeat at the hands of Publius Cornelius Scipio's son (of the same name) at Zama, southwest of Carthage.

Sadly, Fabius did not live to see Carthage's final defeat in the war. The year before the showdown at Zama, he fell ill and died at the age of about seventy-two. As a special token of respect and love for him, the people set aside the usual state-financed funeral given fallen leaders and paid for his burial out of their own pockets, each and every citizen contributing a single coin. "This was not because he was so poor as to need their help," Plutarch explains, "but rather because they felt that they were burying the father of the people. Thus in his death he received the honor and regard which he had earned by the conduct of his life." [31]

CHAPTER 3

Marius: First of the Military Strongmen

Gaius Marius was the most important military reformer of the late Republic. He was also the first Roman to demonstrate how a successful general could achieve political power by gaining the personal allegiance of his soldiers. Another of his distinctions was that he was one of a new breed of Roman leaders, a so-called new man, a nonaristocrat who rose almost solely by hard work and his own merits, finally attaining the coveted rank of consul. Before Marius, the first-century B.C. Roman historian Sallust explains,

although citizens of low birth had access to other state offices, the consulship was still reserved by custom for noblemen, who contrived to pass it on from one to another of their number. A self-made man, however distinguished he might be or however admirable his achievements, was invariably considered unworthy of that honor, almost as if he were unclean.[32]

This traditional state of affairs changed almost overnight thanks to Marius, who broke all precedents by winning the consulship seven times, five of these consecutively (107, 104–100, and 86 B.C.). Defending his character against attacks by aristocratic opponents jealous of his success, he sought and obtained

Marius, who rose, through talent and hard work, from humble beginnings to the pinnacle of Roman military and political power.

the support of everyday Romans who related to and respected him as a self-made man. Addressing the Senate on becoming consul for the first time, he spun a liability into a political asset:

My political opponents, if they make a mistake, can rely for protection on their ancient lineage, the resources of their relatives and marriage connections, and their numerous dependents. My hopes rest only on myself, and I must sustain them only by courage and uprightness; for I have nothing else to trust in. I know, too . . . that fair-minded and patriotic men wish me well because my efforts are serviceable to our country.[33]

Marius's Early Years

Marius was born the son of a farmer in 157 B.C. at Arpinum, about sixty miles southeast of Rome. What little is known of his childhood comes from a brief passage in the *Life of Marius,* by Plutarch, who states that Marius's parents, Marius and Fulcinia, "were entirely undistinguished. They were poor people who lived by the labor of their own hands. For a long time he never saw Rome or had any idea of city life. . . . His upbringing was rough and unfettered, if compared to the polished ways of cities." [34] Sallust picks up the narrative with Marius already a young man:

> Directly [after] he reached military age, he had gone on active service and set himself to learn the art of warfare; for he was not interested in Greek rhetoric [a traditional subject of study in the education of respectable, substantial men] or the elegant accomplishments of a man about town. . . . Protected from demoralizing influences, his character had quickly matured. So when he first presented himself before the Assembly as a candidate for the post of military tribune, though few people knew him by sight, his reputation was quite enough to secure his election by the unanimous choice of all the voting tribes.[35]

That the young Marius possessed courage, physical toughness, and the ability to judge when to forge ahead and when to cut his losses and quit, all essential qualities of a successful military leader, is evident in an anecdote related by Plutarch. Marius had varicose veins in his legs and decided to have a surgeon remove them. Refusing to be tied down, the usual procedure in the days before the discovery of anesthetics to dull the pain, he endured the doctor's cutting without so much as a groan. When the work on the first leg had been completed, Marius inspected it carefully, saw that the improvement was very minor, and declined having the other leg done. "I can see," he said, "that the result does not justify the pain." [36]

Marius (on horse) as a senior general inspecting his troops. The soldier beside him, known as an aquilifer, *carries the* aquila, *a silver eagle signifying Roman power.*

The Jugurthine War

In the years following his tribuneship, the ever active and ambitious Marius gained increasing recognition in powerful circles. In 115 B.C., at the age of forty-two, he became praetor, a high-ranking civil judge (eight of whom were elected each year). That same year, in an effort to increase his prestige further, he married into a patrician family—the Caesars, of the Julii clan. Not yet born at this time was the nephew of his wife, Julia (and therefore Marius's own nephew by marriage), Gaius Julius Caesar, who would later make his own mark on Roman politics and history. Following custom, as a reward for his praetorship Marius served a one-year term as a provincial governor in 114.

All that is known about his handling of the province of Farther Spain (what is now south-central Spain) is that he suppressed some local brigands who had been victimizing the populace.

Not long after Marius's stay in Spain, trouble erupted farther south, in the kingdom of Numidia, occupying what is now Algeria in northwestern Africa. Numidia had been on friendly terms with Rome ever since its colorful king, Masinissa, had aided the Romans in fighting his neighbor, Carthage. In 118, Rome arranged a settlement whereby two young Numidian princes shared the rule of their realm. One of these princes, Jugurtha, soon rejected the settlement, however, and began massacring the Italian residents of the region. Rome's police action against this upstart became known as the Jugurthine War. The first Roman commanders sent to Numidia were unsuccessful in stopping "the lion of the desert," as Jugurtha came to be called; but in 109, a much more capable general, Quintus Metellus, became consul and took charge of the war. As one of Metellus's deputies, Marius made a name for himself in the campaign.

Marius's big break came two years later, when, partly as a result of his own political intriguing, the Assembly elected him consul, and, overriding the Senate's objections, gave him supreme command in place of Metellus. The events that followed not only established Marius as a military force to be reckoned with but also introduced him to the Roman officer who would later become his archenemy. In Numidia, Marius vigorously attacked one enemy stronghold after another, showing himself to be a general of exceptional ability. Nevertheless, he was unable to capture the crafty Jugurtha. Eventually, Marius's lieutenant, Lucius Cornelius Sulla, arranged for one of Jugurtha's allies to betray the Numidian leader. "It was this," Plutarch tells us,

> that sowed the first seed of that irreconcilable and bitter
> hatred between Marius and Sulla which very nearly
> brought Rome to ruin. There were many who, out of envy
> for Marius, gave the whole credit for the affair to Sulla,
> and Sulla himself used to carry a signet ring which he had
> had made on which was engraved the scene of Jugurtha
> being surrendered to him. . . . By constantly using this ring
> he greatly irritated Marius.[37]

"Marius's Mules"

Even while the war against Jugurtha was in progress, Marius was already instituting the military reforms for which he is still famous. He believed that many of the difficulties and failures displayed by the army in this and prior military campaigns were the result of its outmoded and inefficient organization. First, only citizens who owned a certain amount of property were allowed to serve. This meant that many able-bodied and talented men who would have made excellent soldiers were excluded simply because they were poor. Moreover, those who did serve did so for a very short time and for few or no rewards. Marius's modern biographer Phillip Kildahl explains:

> All men recruited . . . were expected to supply their own equipment and, when war was over, to return to their homes without any pension or gratuity other than whatever booty had come their way. Because only the very wealthy could afford full armor, they were expected to do most of the fighting and to bear the heaviest burdens of the war. Those less wealthy who could afford only partial armor served in the second line of battle, and those so limited in funds that they could afford only a sword and shield were assigned to skirmishing.[38]

In overhauling the army, Marius first dropped all property qualifications and accepted volunteers from all classes. This not

In this nineteenth-century drawing, the African rebel Jugurtha is forced to humble himself before Sulla (seated at right).

A fanciful modern drawing depicts Marius, as a young man, sitting in the ruins of Carthage, which the Romans had destroyed only two decades before.

only greatly increased the number of potential recruits, but also initiated profound changes in the character of the military. In the past, the majority of soldiers, especially the well-to-do, looked on military service as a necessary but unpleasant duty; their aim was to discharge that duty as quickly as possible and resume their civilian careers. For the volunteers of Marius's more permanent, professional force, by contrast, serving in the army *was* their career, to which many brought enthusiasm and a sense of purpose and pride.

Part of that pride was in serving under a capable, successful commander, especially one like Marius, a man of common birth like themselves, with whom they inevitably formed a strong bond.

The Germanic Teutones rally for a military campaign. These undisciplined but effective warriors caused the Romans serious casualties before Marius defeated them.

And since the government still refused to provide them pensions when their hitches were over, they increasingly looked to him to supply such rewards. With the aid of a popular politician named Saturninus, Marius eventually arranged for his retired veterans to receive generous land allotments in northern Africa, southern Gaul, Sicily, and Greece. Not surprisingly, he had no trouble in calling on these men later to enforce his will, sometimes violently, on his political opponents. "This intervention by Marius's soldiery was ominous," Michael Grant points out, "for it showed generals of the future they could enlist armies of their own troops and veterans . . . to secure absolute power for themselves."[39]

Among Marius's other reforms was to supply all troops with standard weapons. Especially important in this regard was his introduction of an improved version of the javelin (throwing spear), or *pilum*. The new weapon was equipped with a wooden rivet that broke on impact, preventing an enemy soldier from throwing it back. He also standardized and improved the quality of training and taught the soldiers to carry their own supplies rather than rely on cumbersome baggage-trains of mules that slowed down an army on the march. Plutarch writes:

> There was practice in running and in long marches; and every man was compelled to carry his own baggage and to prepare his own meals. This was the origin of the expression "one of Marius's mules," applied later to any soldier who was a glutton for work and obeyed orders cheerfully and without grumbling.[40]

Intruders in Gaul

Marius's new and improved army proved itself to some degree in the African war, but much more decisively in a more serious emergency that arose in 105 B.C. The Cimbri and Teutones—large, restless Germanic tribes, perhaps numbering in the hundreds of thousands—had recently begun to overrun Narbonensis (or Narbonese), Rome's province in southern Gaul. Two generals, one a consul for that year, engaged the intruders at Arausio (modern Orange), on the southern reaches of the Rhone River, and there suffered the worst Roman defeat since Hannibal's victory at Cannae a century before. A wave of fear now rippled through Italy, for these "barbarians," as the Romans called them, seemed bent on ravaging more than Gaul. "Their courage and daring were irresistible," recalls Plutarch, and

> in their fighting they rushed into battle with the speed of a raging fire; nothing could stand up to them, and all who came in their way were carried off as the . . . spoils of war. . . . Having conquered all who opposed them and having won great quantities of booty, they made up their minds not to settle down anywhere until they had destroyed Rome.[41]

Indeed, at this juncture the only effective force that stood between the invaders and the Italian heartland was Marius and his

43

"mules." Following his second election to the consulship late in 105, he marched northward and, after some tough campaigning, in 102 he crushed the Teutones at Aquae Sextiae, south of Arausio. According to Plutarch:

> The Romans awaited the enemy's attack, then joined with them and checked them as they charged up hill, and then little by little forced them backwards down into the plain. Those [Teutones] in the rear were now pushing in among the natives who were in the front and quickly threw the whole army into confusion. Exposed to attack from two directions, their resistance soon gave way and they broke line and fled. In the pursuit the Romans killed or captured more than a hundred thousand of them, and seized their tents, their wagons, and their property.[42]

The following year, Marius inflicted an even more shattering defeat on the Cimbri near Ferrara, in northern Italy. The successful campaign made Marius the hero of the hour; more importantly, it also afforded him the opportunity to amass unprecedented personal power—politically by his repeated re-election as consul during the crisis, and militarily through his army reforms, which he continued to implement all the while.

Day of Reckoning

For many years Marius remained the most powerful and feared Roman general. But eventually his position was challenged by Sulla, who had in recent years attained much power and prestige of his own, and who still bragged, at Marius's ex-

A likeness of Cornelius Sulla, who made the unprecedented move of declaring himself dictator of Rome in 83 B.C.

pense, about capturing Jugurtha. In 88 B.C., Sulla was elected consul and the Senate assigned him an army to quell a threat to Roman interests in Asia Minor. But the leaders of the popular party, who dominated the Assembly, wanted their own favorite— the tried and true Marius—to lead the eastern campaign.

As tensions between the popular and aristocratic factions swiftly rose, Sulla struck first. He marched an army into the capital and pushed through a law that forbade the Assembly from voting on any measure without the Senate's consent. Having hamstrung the popular party and greatly strengthened the Senate and aristocracy, he departed with his troops for Asia Minor. With Sulla gone, however, his opponents grew bolder. Marius himself eventually entered the city and with the aid of his soldiers and henchmen took control, in the process murdering many of Sulla's aristocratic supporters.

Soon afterward, Marius, now an old man, fell ill and died. The exact circumstances are uncertain; however, Plutarch suggests that

> while walking with his friends after dinner, [he] began to talk about his life; beginning from his early youth he dwelt on all the changes for good or ill which had occurred. . . . After this he said good-bye to his friends, took to his bed and, after seven days, died.[43]

Marius's followers now waited anxiously for the day of reckoning when Sulla would return from the east. That day came, both for them and the Republic, in 83 B.C., as, at the head of his own loyal personal army, Sulla seized the capital by force. Once firmly in control, he took the unprecedented action of making himself dictator for an indefinite term. The rule of the military strongmen, a phenomenon Marius had initiated years before, now began to chip away in earnest at the Republic's already rickety foundations; unbeknownst to all, catastrophic collapse was only a few decades away.

CHAPTER 4

Caesar: Politician, Conqueror, and Dictator

Perhaps the most famous of all Roman figures, without doubt one of the greatest military leaders of all times, and the man who brought the Roman Republic to its knees, Gaius Julius Caesar was born on July 12, 100 B.C. His parents, Gaius and Aurelia, were well-to-do patricians who traced their family lineage back to Julus, a son of the legendary hero Aeneas. Later, to bolster his public image, Caesar himself would claim an even more illustrious ancestry, namely direct descent from Venus, goddess of love. There was no way, of course, for his opponents to challenge this claim, nor, for that matter, for him to prove it. Yet the prestigious offices and titles held by a number of his relatives were real enough and more than sufficient to impress people and help pave his way into the corridors of fame and power. His father served as praetor in 92 and the following year as a provincial governor. Also in 91, his uncle Sextus Julius Caesar was elected consul. And most important of all was his connection to Marius (also his uncle), a political-military figure of towering reputation during the period of Caesar's childhood.

Something Uncanny in His Manner

Of that childhood, little of a concrete nature is known. As a boy he no doubt witnessed or heard firsthand about his uncle Marius's dealings; and as a young man he supported Marius after the aging general took control of Rome in Sulla's absence. When Marius died suddenly in 86 B.C., shortly after obtaining his seventh consulship, Caesar sought a way to retain his position in the popular party (the *populares*) that Marius had headed. The sixteen-year-old accomplished this goal by marrying Cornelia, daughter of the new leader of the party, Cornelius Cinna.

Cozying up to the popular party proved to be one of Caesar's few political miscalculations. When the aristocratic Sulla returned in 83 and seized the capital, he killed thousands of *populares* in a frightening, bloody purge. "He also condemned anyone who sheltered or attempted to save a person whose name was on the lists [of the condemned]," writes Plutarch. "Death was the penalty for such acts of humanity."[44] Probably because Caesar was a fellow aristocrat, Sulla at first spared him. But when the dictator demanded that the youth divorce his wife as a way of renouncing allegiance to the *populares*, Caesar refused and was forced into hiding. Their meeting had disquieted Sulla, who had looked the young man in the eye and recognized a potentially dangerous opponent. "There are many Mariuses in this fellow Caesar," he warned.[45]

Sulla did not live to see this warning confirmed. He died unexpectedly in 78, allowing the senators and consuls to regain control, and for the time being Rome returned to normal. Caesar reasoned that the time was now right for him to begin making a name for himself. One way he did so was to take full advantage of his imposing physical appearance. The later Roman historian Suetonius describes him as

Unlike Marius, who came from an undistinguished family, Julius Caesar (pictured) was born an aristocrat.

> tall, fair, and well-built, with a rather broad face and keen, dark-brown eyes. . . . He was something of a dandy, always keeping his head carefully trimmed and shaved; and . . . having certain other hairy parts of his body plucked with tweezers.[46]

Caesar also threw lavish parties and did favors for acquaintances, calculating correctly that this was a proven way to build a strong political reputation. According to Plutarch:

> He had an ability to make himself liked which was remarkable in one of his age, and he was very much in the

good graces of the ordinary citizen because of his easy manners and the friendly way in which he mixed with people. Then there [was] . . . a certain splendor about his whole way of life; all this made him gradually more and more important politically.[47]

Yet his personality also had a distant quality, an aloofness that rarely turned these impressed acquaintances into true friends. "There was something uncanny in his manner," remarks his modern biographer Matthias Gelzer, "which made his enemies suspicious of any overture from him and on the other hand impeded genuine friendship."[48]

Up the Political Ladder

Perhaps Caesar's aloofness was a calculated effort rather than a character flaw; from the very beginning, after all, his goal was to

attain ultimate power; so perhaps he thought it best not to become too attached to people he might later have to turn on and destroy. In any case, he began his methodical climb up the political ladder in 69 B.C. by securing the office of quaestor, one of Rome's twenty financial administrators.[49] The following year he married Pompeia, an aristocratic young woman related to the former dictator Sulla. Caesar's first wife, Cornelia, whom he had grown to love, had died suddenly three years before. After her passing, he no longer concerned himself with the emotional side of marriage. The union with Pompeia was strictly one of convenience; in plain fact, he needed a lot of money to finance his drive for power, and her family was one of the richest in Rome.

While serving as aedile in 65 B.C., Caesar, hoping to impress people, spent a great deal of his own money staging public games and shows.

Caesar put the extra money to good use in his next public post, that of aedile, one of the officials charged with maintaining public buildings, markets, and overseeing public games and other entertainments. He outdid himself in

The senators stand in judgment over members of Catiline's failed conspiracy to take over the government. Caesar gained notoriety by recommending leniency for the traitors.

the job, staging the most spectacular gladiatorial fights Rome had ever witnessed. That success made Caesar a household name and significantly contributed to his election as praetor in 63.

The results of the consular race in that election soon brought an unexpected national crisis that served to further increase Caesar's prominence. Catiline, a debt-ridden aristocrat with a reputation for shady dealings, lost the consulship to the popular lawyer and orator Cicero and soon afterward hatched a deadly scheme to gain revenge. The plan, including the murder of the consuls and seizure of the government, failed. In the heat of the moment, Cicero and several senators advocated that Catiline and his fellow conspirators be executed immediately, without benefit of a trial, a clear violation of Roman law. Suddenly perceiving a chance to enhance his own image at their expense, Caesar asked for permission to address the Senate and, receiving it, declared:

> You, Fathers of the Senate, must beware of letting the [conspirators'] guilt have more weight with you than your own dignity. . . . I should advise limiting ourselves to such penalties as the law has established. . . . This is rather my advice: that their goods be confiscated and they themselves be kept imprisoned.

The members of the powerful political partnership later known as the First Triumvirate—Gnaeus Pompey, Julius Caesar, and Marcus Crassus—plot the murders of their opponents.

He concluded by warning that people "remember only that which happens last," meaning that after the conspirators' deeds were forgotten, Romans would remember only the senators' rash and harsh judgment.[50] This prediction turned out to be accurate. Cicero and the others ignored his plea, executed the prisoners, and enjoyed momentary popularity; however, in time public opinion turned against the Senate for its abuse of established law and tradition; and for trying to stop that abuse, Caesar gained the image of a wise and courageous leader.

Thereafter, relations cooled between Caesar and many senators, who saw him as a threat and wanted to keep him from gaining more power, especially the consulship. But he shrewdly outmaneuvered them. In the summer of 60, he engineered a political alliance with the two most powerful men in Rome, military general Gnaeus Pompey and wealthy financier Marcus Crassus. Singly, each lacked the resources to dominate the Senate; but by combining their wealth and influence, Caesar proposed, they could conceivably manipulate the government to their own ends. Their partnership, which later became known as the First Triumvirate ("rule of three"), proved devastatingly powerful. With Crassus's and Pompey's backing, Caesar easily became consul (for the year 59) and used, or more accurately misused, his authority to intimidate and silence almost all opposition.

The Conquest of Gaul

Though Caesar now dominated the political scene in the capital, he realized that achieving such power was one thing and holding onto it indefinitely quite another. After his consulship ended, he reasoned, his opponents would surely try to get even. For the moment he had Pompey's troops to protect him and enforce his will, but what if Pompey, who was also an ambitious man, decided suddenly to turn his might *against* Caesar? Clearly, in order to maintain his power base when no longer a consul, Caesar needed a tool that Marius, Sulla, and Pompey all had exploited—an army more loyal to him than to the state.

One way to acquire such a force was to become governor of a province. There, he could raise whatever troops he needed and then launch a major military campaign, during which his men would become battle hardened and devoted to him.

With this plan in mind, Caesar used his consular influence to gain the governorship of Cisalpine Gaul, consisting mainly of northern Italy's Po Valley. Then, just before his term as consul ended, he managed to get his hands on the Gallic province of Narbonensis, too. When he took charge of these provinces in 58 B.C., he found about twenty-four thousand troops at his disposal and immediately began raising more recruits. He

Caesar is cheered by his troops after addressing them. His close bond with these men contributed greatly to his military successes.

needed as large a force as he could muster, for his real interest was not in administering Narbonensis but in conquering the lands stretching westward and northward from it. The Romans saw this region of Transalpine Gaul, encompassing what is now most of France and Belgium, as vast, wild, and mysterious. Caesar described what little he knew of it in the famous opening lines of his

Commentary on the Gallic War, the personal journal he kept of his campaigns:

> The country of Gaul consists of three separate parts, one of which is inhabited by the Belgae, one by the Aquitani, and one by the people whom we call "Gauls" but who are known in their own language as "Celts." The three peoples differ from one another in language, customs and laws. . . . The toughest soldiers come from the Belgae. This is because they are farthest away from the culture and civilized way of life of the Roman province [Narbonensis].[51]

Fully accepting the prevailing, highly arrogant Roman attitude that these uncultured tribesmen were barbarians who would one day be thankful for having been Romanized, Caesar launched campaign after campaign against them. During these conquests, which spanned almost eight years, he consistently displayed not only strategic brilliance but raw courage and amazing physical prowess, as well. "Caesar was a most skillful swordsman and horseman," Suetonius states,

> and showed surprising powers of endurance. He . . . went bareheaded in sun and rain alike, and could travel for long distances at incredible speed . . . and often he arrived at his destination before the messengers whom he had sent ahead to announce his approach.[52]

Such actions won him the admiration and devotion of his troops, one of his chief immediate goals. He also fulfilled his other goal of gaining prestige and power by greatly expanding the Roman realm, for by the end of 51 he had subdued nearly all of Transalpine Gaul. Overall, Caesar had fought more than thirty major battles, captured over eight hundred towns, and killed over a million people, an impressive or despicable record, depending on one's point of view.

Triumph in Death

Returning from his Gallic conquests in 50 B.C., Caesar camped his army in Cisalpine Gaul and contemplated his next move. At that moment the capital was in a state of turmoil. Since Crassus's death in 53 the triumvirate had fallen apart; Pompey, the consuls, and the Senate each now vied for authority, all of them viewing Caesar's new and formidable military might with much anxiety. In a desperate attempt to remove Caesar's fangs, the Senate ordered him to lay down command of his armies and, when he refused, relieved

Caesar leads his troops across the Rubicon River. The fateful act ignited a destructive civil war that raged for five years.

him of his governorship. He then made a fateful decision. On January 10, 49, he reached the Rubicon River, the border between his province and Italy proper. "We may still draw back," he told his officers, "but once across that little bridge, we shall have to fight it out. . . . Let us . . . follow where [the gods] beckon, in vengeance on our double-dealing enemies. The die is cast." [53] With these words, Caesar led his men across the river in open defiance of the Senate, plunging the Roman world into a devastating civil war.

As the bloody conflict opened, Caesar's forces marched on Rome, inducing Pompey and a large number of senators to flee Italy for Greece. On August 9 of the following year, on the plain of Pharsalus in east-central Greece, Caesar's army, outnumbered nearly two to one, won a stunning victory over Pompey and the senatorial forces. Thereafter Caesar racked up one victory after another, defeating adversaries in Egypt, Asia Minor, Africa, and Spain. When he finally and triumphantly entered the capital in September 45, he was the undisputed master of the Roman world and quite literally the most powerful human being who had ever lived.

Now firmly in control of the government, Caesar surprised those who saw him as nothing more than a brutal warmonger by proving himself a civil administrator of extraordinary skill, perhaps even of

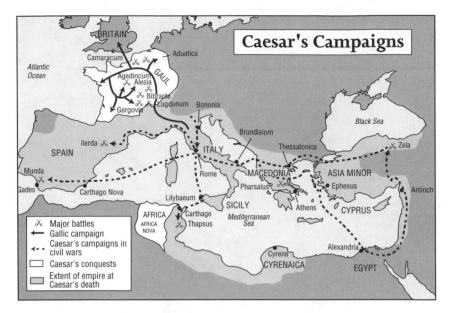

Caesar's Campaigns

Major battles
Gallic campaign
Caesar's campaigns in civil wars
Caesar's conquests
Extent of empire at Caesar's death

genius. His adept handling of problems ranging from the national debt to an inaccurate and confusing calendar suggested that he might lead Rome into a bright and constructive future.[54]

But this was not to be, for in his rise to power Caesar had made many enemies, and he now proceeded to make even more. He firmly believed that the best way to achieve permanent peace and prosperity was to abandon many of the old republican ways and place most state power in the hands of a benevolent dictator. Accordingly, in February 44 he took the bold and fateful step of declaring himself dictator *perpetuo,* "for life." Fearing that his absolute rule might spell the end of their beloved Republic, a group of senators stabbed him to death in the Senate on March 15 of that year. The conspirators naively believed, writes biographer Christian Meier, "that once the tyrant was removed they would have achieved their aim . . . [and] that the Republic would come into its own again. . . . They had understood nothing of the conditions that made his ascendancy possible."[55]

Indeed, the assassins' rash act did not bring back the Republic. It only succeeded in igniting another ruinous civil war, from which eventually emerged the same sort of benevolent dictator Caesar had envisioned. By leaving behind the blueprint from which his immediate successors constructed the immensely successful Roman Empire, the irrepressible Caesar had attained even greater triumph in death than in life.

CHAPTER 5

Cicero: Last Champion of the Republic

More is known about Marcus Tullius Cicero, the great statesman who gave his life trying to preserve the disintegrating Roman Republic, than about any other person of the ancient world. His prominence as a lawyer, orator, consul, senator, patriot, and prodigious and gifted writer loomed large in the Roman consciousness, both in his own and later eras. After his death his speeches became textbooks of oratory and his ideas and deeds were retold and discussed by scholars and writers of all disciplines and nationalities. Many, including his own freed slave, Tiro, wrote biographies of him. Sadly, most of these are lost; however, Plutarch managed to collect a fair share of their contents in his own *Life of Cicero*, which has survived.

Most of our unique knowledge of Cicero, however, comes from the great man himself. His mammoth literary output, including fifty-eight lengthy speeches, more than eight hundred letters, and some two thousand pages of philosophical and rhetorical tracts, is a treasure trove of information about himself, his friends, his society, and the Roman character. The letters are especially telling and timeless. About half of them are addressed to his close friend, Titus Pomponius Atticus, to whom he reveals himself with unparalleled frankness. Feeling melancholy and lazy while on a trip, for instance, the usually energetic Cicero admits that

> I have fallen so in love with idleness that I can't tear myself from it. So I either enjoy myself with my books . . . or else count the waves [at the seashore]. . . . I am debating . . . spending the rest of my life here. . . . This is the very place for me to play the politician, for . . . I am sick of [the politicians] in Rome. So I will compose a private memoir, which I will read only to you.[56]

This was but a momentary lapse for Cicero, who, though often "sick of" the political game in the capital, could not bear to stay away from it for very long. There he "played the politician," as he tirelessly, and in the final analysis vainly, attempted to prop up the traditional government as it crumbled around him.

A Very Human Personality

Rome's last republican champion was born on January 3, 106 B.C., in Arpinum, the same town that produced Marius. The two men were distantly connected: Marius had adopted the son of the brother-in-law of Cicero's paternal grandfather; and Cicero attended elementary school with Marius's son. While at that school, Cicero wrote a poem (only fragments of which survive) praising the renowned general, of whom, naturally enough, all the locals were duly proud.

Cicero composes a letter. A gifted writer, he turned out hundreds of letters, speeches, and philosophical works.

Yet as Cicero matured, it became clear that Arpinum's two native sons were nothing alike. Marius was uneducated and rough in manners, opposed the patricians, and thrived on army life and war; Cicero, on the other hand, was supremely educated and well bred, became the leader of the patricians, and thoroughly detested war. Perhaps the most appealing part of Cicero's character, so evident in his correspondence, was that he was always striving for intellectual and spiritual growth. Continually he tried to improve himself, to correct what were no more than very human faults with which people in all places and times can readily identify. As Ciceronian scholar John Rolfe puts it:

> All in all, Cicero was . . . a human, not a heroic personality. He was warm-hearted and emotional, a good friend but always a good hater and inclined even to be vindictive. . . . He was quick to receive impressions and inclined to believe what he himself wished to be true. His life . . . is particularly inspiring because all his defects were nat-

ural, all his merits the result of education and efforts at self-improvement.[57]

His ardent desire to succeed, to get ahead and make his mark in Roman social and political circles, is illustrated in a charming episode recounted by Plutarch, which also captures Cicero's well-known sense of humor. The question was whether people would take seriously a public figure whose name was a form of the word *cicer*, meaning chickpea.

> When he first entered politics and stood for office . . . his friends thought that he ought either to drop or change his name. He said that he was going to do his best to make the name of Cicero . . . famous . . . . [Later] when he made an offering to the gods of some silver plate, he had his first two names, Marcus and Tullius, inscribed on the plate and then, by way of a joke, told the craftsman to engrave a chick-pea instead of the third name.[58]

Ambition and wit alone, however, were not enough to ensure success in the competitive world of Roman power politics. Oratorical skills and legal knowledge were a must, and in this regard Cicero was fortunate to study with the leading experts in both areas. The legendary Apollonius Molo, from the Greek island of Rhodes, taught him rhetoric, the art of persuasive speaking, and the greatest lawyer of the day, Mucius Scaevola, tutored him in the law.

Under the guidance of these men, Cicero's considerable innate talents quickly matured and his rise to public prominence was nothing less than meteoric. "When he took up his work as an advocate [lawyer]," Plutarch tells us, "it was by no means slowly or gradually that he

This famous bust of Cicero in his later years captures his keen intelligence and noble bearing, qualities that contributed to his rise to power.

came to the top. He blazed out into fame at once and far surpassed all his competitors at the bar [i.e., in the legal profession]."[59] In 80 B.C., when he was twenty-six, the young advocate attracted much attention in his first big case, defending a man named Roscius, who had been accused of killing his own father. Roscius's prosecutor was an associate of Sulla, then absolute dictator; it was well known that Sulla wanted to see the accused man convicted, so Cicero was risking much by representing Roscius. Prudently, after Cicero won the case he took an extended holiday in Athens to avoid possible retaliation by Sulla.

Following Sulla's death in 78, Cicero returned to Rome and resumed his career. In addition to his legal work, the young man began a political rise that in many ways paralleled that of his con-

A nineteenth-century drawing shows Cicero delivering a speech from a speaker's platform in the Roman Forum (main square).

temporary and sometimes opponent, Caesar. Cicero served as quaestor in 75, became a senator in 74, and was elected aedile in 69. Shortly before his aedileship, he acquired much added fame and prestige in his vigorous prosecution of Gaius Verres, governor of the province of Sicily, who stood accused of mismanagement of funds and other shady tactics while in office. Cicero gave his all to the case, partly because of the challenge of grappling with Verres's lawyer, Quintus Hortensius, then seen as the greatest orator of the day; but also because Cicero was a patriotic man who believed in the republican system and genuinely hated to see it exploited and corrupted, as it had increasingly come to be, by rich, powerful men. "A belief has taken root which is having a fatal effect on our nation," he told the judges in the case,

> and which to us who are senators, in particular, threatens grave peril. . . . It is this: that in these courts . . . even the worst criminal will never be convicted provided that he has money. . . . Here is a man whose life and actions the world has already condemned—yet whose enormous fortune, according to his own loudly expressed hopes, has already brought him acquittal! . . . [The people's] eyes are upon you now. They are watching to see [if you will support] the demands of our conscience and law.[60]

Cicero went on to attack Verres's entire public record and subsequently won the case.[61]

The prestige gained from the Verres case helped Cicero become praetor in 66. Many people found him refreshing and reassuring as a representative of old-fashioned Roman values of honesty, unselfish service to the state, and duty to country, at a time when government was increasingly beset by self-serving, power-hungry individuals and groups. As he himself later described it, the ideal public servant

> should carry with [him] greatness of spirit and . . . lead a dignified and self-consistent life. . . . If anyone is entering public life, let him beware of thinking only of the honor that it brings. . . . At the same time, let him take care not to lose heart too readily through discouragement nor yet to be overconfident through ambition.[62]

From Hero to Exile

Cicero's leadership qualities and devout patriotism shone most brightly in the crisis that gripped Rome in the months following

Exposing the conspiracy, Cicero rails against Catiline, who stands alone (in background at right), shunned by the other senators.

his election as consul in 63 B.C.—the infamous Catilinian conspiracy. On learning that Catiline was plotting to kill him and his fellow consul, Antonius, and then take over the government, Cicero acted swiftly and boldly. In a magnificent speech to the Senate, with Catiline himself sitting before him in the chamber, Cicero exposed the scheme. "In the name of heaven, Catiline, how long will you exploit our patience?" he began.

> Surely your insane activities cannot escape our retaliation forever! Are there to be no limits to this swaggering, ungovernable recklessness? . . . You must be well aware that your plot has been detected. Now that every single person in this place knows all about your conspiracy, you cannot fail to realize it is doomed. . . . What a scandalous commentary on our age and its standards! For the Senate knows all about these things. . . . And yet this man [Catiline] still lives! Lives? He walks right into the Senate. He . . . watches and notes and marks down with his gaze each one of us he plots to assassinate.[63]

Catiline at first denied the charges, then lost his temper and began insulting Cicero. At that, according to Sallust's account,

> the whole house shouted him down with cries of "Enemy!" and "Traitor!" At this time he flew into a towering rage. "Since I am surrounded by foes," he cried, "and hounded to desperation, I will check the fire that threatens to consume me by pulling everything down about your ears!" [64]

But Catiline had severely overestimated his own abilities and powers. Early in 62, Antonius attacked and defeated the small army the would-be usurper was raising for his coup, killing him in the process. Then Cicero ordered Catiline's accomplices, without benefit of the trials guaranteed by law, to be strangled to death in what Sallust termed a "filthy, dark, and foul-smelling" prison cell. [65]

For rescuing the government, Cicero was applauded as a hero and acclaimed "Father of His Country." However, his denial of the conspirators' legal rights was an error in judgment that later came back to haunt him. Cicero, of course, opposed the triumvirate (the coalition of Caesar, Pompey, and Crassus in 60) and continued to be a thorn in the side of the strongmen who ran roughshod over the state. In 58, shortly before Caesar left for Gaul, one of his chief associates, the ambitious and disreputable Clodius, succeeded temporarily in silencing Cicero. Clodius used his influence to help pass a law calling for the banishment of anyone who had caused the death of a Roman citizen without a regular trial; and to avoid certain conviction, Cicero went into voluntary exile in Greece.

A Blessing in Death?

Many of Cicero's friends and associates visited and tried to comfort him while he was away; but as Plutarch wrote, "he remained for most of the time miserable . . . keeping his eyes fixed, like a distressed lover, on Italy." [66] Luckily for Cicero, Clodius soon irritated both the Senate and Pompey so much that they silenced *him*, and Cicero was allowed to return home after an absence of some sixteen months. [67] But though at first elated to be back in the political arena, in the years that followed Cicero became increasingly disillusioned. Time and again he found his efforts to reinstate the Senate's authority impeded by Caesar and Pompey. And when civil war erupted in 49, Cicero held himself and his colleagues partly to blame, mainly for their failure to stop the rise of the generals in the first place. "Do you see," he asked in a letter to Atticus, "the kind of man into whose hands the state has fallen? . . . It pains me to think of the mistakes and wrongs of ours that are responsible for this."[68] Later, in 46, by which time Caesar had become a virtual dictator, Cicero retired from politics, feeling his voice was no longer effective.

However, in 44, after Caesar's assassination and the assumption of his dictatorial powers by his associate, Marcus Antonius (Mark Antony), Cicero felt compelled to reenter the political fray. The sixty-two-year-old statesman hoped that he could help rid Rome of Antony, an alcoholic and inept administrator, and clear the way for a renewal of the traditional system. To this end, Cicero composed several speeches denouncing Antony, which became known as the Philippics.[69] In the first, he called on Antony to act reasonably and justly: "Change your ways, I entreat you. Remember your ances-

Another modern rendering of Cicero addressing a crowd. His speeches against Antony were among his most powerful.

tors and govern our country in such a way that your fellow citizens will rejoice that you were born."[70] In the second, more daring and ferocious speech, Cicero called his opponent a gangster, a prostitute, a spiritual bankrupt, a "drunken, sex-ridden wreck," and a "loathsome gladiator," adding in the closing lines,

> When I was a young man I defended our state: in my old age I shall not abandon it. Having scorned the swords of Catiline, I shall not be intimidated by yours. On the contrary, I would gladly offer my own body, if my death could redeem the freedom of our nation.[71]

Unfortunately for Cicero, Antony took him up on this offer, and at the cost, rather than the restoration, of Roman freedoms. In the winter of 43, Antony joined with a general named Lepidus and Caesar's adopted son, Octavian, to form a new triumvirate. Their first order of business was to eradicate their enemies; not surprisingly, Cicero's name appeared at the top of Antony's list. The triumvir's henchman caught up with the great orator at his country house at Astura, on the seacoast about fifty miles south of Rome. "In that characteristic posture of his," Plutarch tells it, "with his chin resting on his left hand, [he] looked steadfastly at his murderers. . . . Most of those who stood by covered their faces while [they] were killing him."[72] At Antony's orders, they cut off his head and hands and nailed them to a platform in Rome's main square.

Mark Antony, the crude but capable soldier who eventually ordered Cicero's murder.

In a very real sense, the Republic died with Cicero, murdered, as he was, by callous, greedy men interested only in furthering their own ambitions and agendas. He never quite understood how they could so disregard the good of the community that had nurtured them. "Who, in God's name, could possibly derive advantage from murdering his country?" he had once written. "Of all murders that is the most hideous and repulsive."[73] Perhaps it was a blessing that he did not live to see the coming of the Empire and *Pax Romana*; for as one of his modern biographers suggests, "the peace of Augustus would have seemed like a pall of death to the old champion of the free Republic."[74]

CHAPTER 6

Augustus: Architect of the Empire

Gaius Octavius the Younger, who would later be called Augustus and reign over the known world as the first and arguably greatest Roman emperor, was born in Rome on September 23, 63 B.C. Known simply as Octavian throughout his youth and early manhood, he was short, very slight of build, and prone to sickness. According to Suetonius, "His body is said to have been marred by blemishes of various sorts. . . . He had a weakness in his left hip, thigh, and leg, which occasionally gave him the suspicion of a limp . . . [and he] survived several grave and dangerous illnesses at different periods."[75]

A bust of Augustus as a young boy, when he first acquired the nickname of Octavian.

Fatefully, Octavian's great-uncle, the powerful and influential Julius Caesar, early took a liking to him. In September 47, shortly after his victory at Pharsalus in Greece, Caesar offered the sixteen-year-old a position on his military staff; however, Octavian's mother, Atia, fearing the campaign would be too dangerous for someone so young, refused to let her son accept the post. As a consolation to his disappointed nephew, when he returned victorious from that campaign, Caesar gave Octavian some military decorations and allowed him to march in his victory parade. The general next invited the young man to accompany him on a campaign in Spain. A bout of illness kept Octavian from joining Caesar right away, but eventually, after an adventurous journey that included surviving a shipwreck, he caught up with his uncle and the two returned to Rome together at the campaign's conclusion.

Caesar's Heir

During the winter of 45–44, Caesar, apparently as part of an effort to groom Octavian for an illustrious political career, sent the young man to Greece to study under the distinguished scholar Apollodorus of Pergamum. The parting between the uncle and nephew, who had by now grown very close, was to be their last contact. A few months later, Octavian received the news of Caesar's murder in the Senate. This event and the turbulence that followed profoundly changed the course of Octavian's life, for he suddenly found himself thrust into the limelight as a participant in the power struggle that erupted after Caesar's death.

Octavian, now nineteen, was on his way back to Rome when he learned that Caesar's will had been opened; the dictator had left him three-quarters of his considerable estate, and had also legally adopted him as his son. Shrewdly realizing that his dead relative's name still held prestige and authority, especially among Caesar's soldiers, the young man immediately began calling himself Gaius Julius Caesar. "In one bold stroke," comments scholar Henry Rowell, Octavian "had created for himself a reservoir of power. He had made himself the person around whom all those who were loyal to Caesar's memory and incensed by his unworthy end could rally." [76]

The potential of Octavian's calculating mind did not escape Cicero, who met the young man shortly afterward at a social

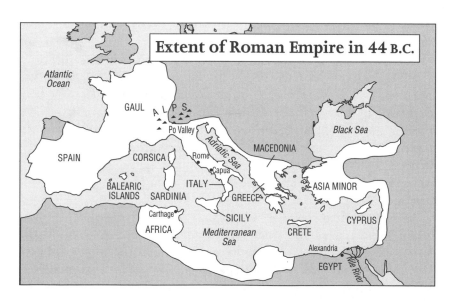

Extent of Roman Empire in 44 B.C.

gathering and recognized immediately that he was not as harmless as he appeared. "Octavian is here with us on terms of respect and friendship," the disquieted old senator wrote to Atticus.

> His people address him as Caesar, but Philippus [Octavian's stepfather] does not, and so I do not either. I hold that it is impossible for a loyal citizen to do so. We are surrounded by so many who threaten death to our friends. . . . What do you think will happen when this boy comes to Rome? . . . Unless I am much mistaken, [we] shall be crushed.[77]

Much less savvy than Cicero, Mark Antony, Caesar's chief military associate, failed to recognize Octavian's abilities and treated the young man with disdain when he arrived in the capital to collect his inheritance. According to Plutarch:

> Antony was at first inclined to despise Octavian as a mere boy, and told him that he must be out of his mind, adding the warning that a young man who possessed few influential friends and little experience of the world would find it a crushing burden to accept the inheritance and act as Caesar's executor. Octavian was quite unmoved by this argument and continued to demand the money, while Antony for his part did everything possible to humiliate him.[78]

Wise Beyond His Years

Far from humiliated and cowed by Antony, the wily Octavian wasted no time in using his formidable new name and fortune. Acquiring the backing of a small army of Caesar's troops, he forced the much surprised and unprepared Antony to flee Rome. In his own later synopsis of his life and deeds, the *Res gestae* (literally, "things done"), Octavian declared matter-of-factly, "When I was nineteen I collected an army on my own account and at my own expense, by the help of which I liberated the state from the tyranny of a [political] faction."[79] The "faction" to which he referred was, of course, Antony. Soon afterward, Octavian himself became a faction to be reckoned with as the Senate grudgingly recognized the reality of his military power by making him what was in effect a third consul for the year 43 B.C.

Octavian's next move showed again that he was politically wise beyond his years. The young man realized that Antony would surely raise his own army to fight him and that other powerful generals, the strongest being Marcus Lepidus, would also challenge him for pieces of the Roman pie. And so, partly to gain recognition as their equal, in the winter of 43, Octavian boldly approached these men and suggested forming a new triumvirate. They accepted. According to the second-century A.D. historian Appian:

> The three of them sat down together, with Octavian in the center. . . . They met for two days, from dawn to dusk. . . . The three distributed the Roman empire among themselves. . . . They also decided to put their private enemies to death . . . to prevent them causing trouble. . . . Such were their decisions, which they recorded in writing, and Octavian, as consul, read them out (with the exception of the list of those who were to die) to the soldiers, who raised cheers of triumph.[80]

Octavian as a young man. Most Roman leaders at first made the mistake of underestimating his abilities.

Unfortunately for Rome and posterity, among the "private enemies" the three men coldly eliminated in the coming weeks was the great Cicero.

The triumvirs next dealt with Caesar's assassins. Led by the popular senators Brutus and Cassius, the surviving conspirators had fled to Greece and raised a large army loyal to the Senate and Republic. In October 42, Antony's and Octavian's forces smashed that army on the plain of Philippi, in northern Greece. Distraught and humiliated, Brutus and Cassius committed suicide, and the last hope of restoring the Republic died with them.

Octavian's battles were not over, however. History seemed to repeat itself as the Second Triumvirate, like the first, steadily disintegrated. First Octavian and Antony pushed the weaker Lepidus aside. Then they faced off in yet another round of civil strife, in which Octavian defended Italy and Rome's western territories against Antony, who held sway over the Roman lands and troops of the eastern Mediterranean. Supporting Antony in his bid for ultimate power was his lover, Cleopatra VII, queen of Egypt, who threw her country's vast resources of money and grain behind the effort. But though their forces were formidable, the lovers had met their match in Octavian. Aided by his friend, the gifted military leader Marcus Agrippa, Octavian decisively defeated them at Actium on September 2, 31 B.C., finally ending Rome's destructive cycle of civil wars.

The Exalted One

These events left Octavian, now thirty-two, the most powerful figure in the Roman world. Like his adoptive father, he wanted to use that power to bring about constructive and lasting change, an endeavor that would require significantly restructuring Rome's old government. Octavian knew full well that instituting such drastic change while maintaining his absolute authority would not be an easy task. The trick would be to find a way of wielding dictatorial power without appearing to be too ambitious or tyrannical, a political tightrope act that even the great Caesar had failed to master.

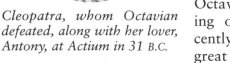

As he deliberated on his strategy, Octavian enjoyed a private reading of the *Georgics*, poems recently completed by his friend, the great writer Virgil. The first section contained a prayer asking the gods to preserve the life of the man who appeared to be the war-weary Roman world's only hope for peace:

Cleopatra, whom Octavian defeated, along with her lover, Antony, at Actium in 31 B.C.

> Oh Gods of our fathers . . . do not hold back this young man hastening to help this unbalanced century! For long enough we have paid with our blood . . . for everywhere good and bad are confused. . . . Wicked Mars [god of war] rages throughout the whole world.[81]

Virgil's words faithfully captured the feelings of most of his fellow Romans. Tired of the suffering, destruction, and uncertainty the many years of civil strife had brought, they longed for peace and the prosperity and happiness it promised.

To gain that peace, they were now willing to follow the lead of one powerful individual, as long as he was capable, fair, and loyal to Rome and its cherished ideals. And most saw Octavian, who had managed to restore order, as that individual. He himself could not help but be moved by their gratitude and hopeful expectation that he had the strength and vision to lead them into a more harmonious age. To that end, in the course of the next few years he slowly and shrewdly consolidated a wide array of the former Republic's powers, always in what appeared to be full accordance with established Roman law and tradition. He did not attempt to confer any powers or titles on himself. Indeed, no attempt was needed, since the senators were more than happy to do so. They now believed as he did that a benign dictator ruling in the Republic's name could bring order and stability to Rome. In a splendid ceremony held on January 16, 27 B.C., they thanked him for "saving the country," and presented him with a laurel wreath, a symbol of honor and glory; then they decreed that henceforth he would be called by the majestic title of Augustus, the "exalted one." As a further honor, the Roman fathers officially changed the month known as *Sextilis* to *Augustus* (now August).[82]

Another important title Augustus already held was that of *Imperator*, or supreme commander, given him by his troops in 43. In time, the term *imperator* would evolve into the word *emperor*. But in his own lifetime, Augustus was always careful to avoid being called emperor, lord, "your highness," or any other title suggestive of kingship, a political concept the Romans despised. He preferred instead the unofficial and more modest name of *princeps*, meaning "first citizen." This gave the impression that he considered himself to be no better than the average Roman. And thereafter he

An idealized portrait of Augustus and his wife, Livia, who was known for her intelligence and generosity.

bolstered his image as a simple man of the people by living, with his wife, Livia, in a small, modestly furnished house and rejecting the usual lavish lifestyle of the wealthy and powerful.

Building on the Ruins of the Past

Augustus accepted the honors his countrymen had bestowed on him in a speech emphasizing his new image of extreme modesty and sincerity. "May I be privileged to build firm and lasting foundations for the Government of the State," he declared. "May I also achieve the reward to which I aspire: that of being known as the author of the best possible Constitution, and of carrying with me, when I die, the hope that these foundations which I have established for the State will abide secure." [83] Just how much of this new benign image was sincere and how much was a political ploy will never be known. What is certain is that during his more than forty years in power he kept his promises to rule justly and constructively and to build a strong and peaceful country. Indeed, the concept of positive reform—of healing the nation's wounds, of building anew, and of restoring lost values—became the hallmark of his long reign.

This policy of creating something new and better on the ruins of the past was most evident in Augustus's impressive public building programs. At the beginning of his reign, Rome was already a large, populous, and important city. But it was old, dirty, unattractive, and had many poorly constructed apartment buildings that often collapsed, killing and maiming many. In Augustus's view, this was hardly a fitting centerpiece for his new imperial order. The Roman Empire needed a capital that would stand as an example of the wealth, nobility, civility, and other "superior" qualities of the Mediterranean's so-called master race. At Augustus's direction, therefore, the city of Rome underwent a mighty burst of urban renewal and large-scale municipal reorganization. As Suetonius sums it up: "Aware that the city was architecturally unworthy of her position as capital of the Roman Empire . . . Augustus so improved her appearance that he could justifiably boast: 'I found Rome built of bricks; I leave her clothed in marble.'" [84]

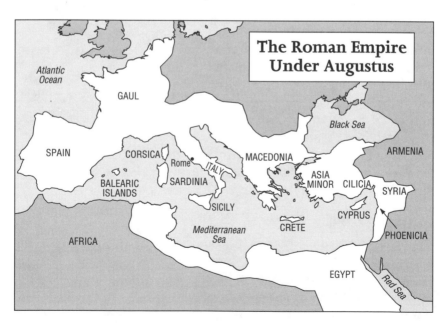

70

Augustus also significantly reorganized and improved the military. Although Marius's reforms had made the troops more professional and provided the opportunity for longer hitches, most leaders of the late Republic continued to raise armies for a given war and disband them at the conclusion of the fighting. Augustus abandoned this system and created a true standing army; he also took care to provide the troops with adequate rewards and pensions to keep them more loyal to him and the state than to their generals. In addition, he built two large imperial navies and several smaller provincial navies. The land and naval forces he created successfully defended the Empire and fought its wars for several centuries to come.[85]

The Prima Porta statue of Augustus portrays him as a serene and majestic ruler.

Augustus's achievements included the creation of a police force for the capital city, substantial and efficient administrative and tax reforms, and steadfast financial and moral support for the arts and literature. Overall, he became such a constructive, effective, and beloved ruler that when he died on August 19, A.D. 14, at the age of seventy-six, the Roman nation grieved more solemnly than it had mourned any past leader. Over a hundred thousand people, many of them weeping openly, marched in his magnificent funeral procession, at the climax of which a lone eagle was released, symbolizing his soul ascending to heaven.

Augustus was truly one of the most remarkable rulers in human history. As a young man he had risen ruthlessly through the corridors of power to become an all-powerful dictator. But unlike most other absolute rulers, once he achieved that position he displayed uncommon wisdom, compassion, and justice. He showed, says Henry Rowell,

> what one great man can do through force and persuasion . . . deed and word, reality and image. He could not turn back time [and erase his youthful mistakes], but he could, and did, place the mark of his greatness in an enduring fashion on the mother city of the Western civilized world.[86]

CHAPTER 7

Nero: Egotist and Enemy of the People

If Augustus had lived to see the reign of his great-great-grandson Nero, the architect of the Empire would not have been at all pleased. Perhaps more than any other of Augustus's immediate successors, Nero personified the opposite of those admirable character traits the first emperor came to stand for. Whereas Augustus had been humble, considerate and humane, simple and unassuming in manner, and morally conservative, Nero was self-centered, callous and cruel, extravagant and flamboyant in manner, and morally depraved. Over the centuries, Nero's brutal reign has come to symbolize the misuse of great power, and numerous despicable acts, some of them factual, others exaggerated or fictitious, have been attributed to him.

Virtuous Intentions

What is much less well known is that Nero did not start out as a murderous despot and that indeed at first it appeared to all that he might become a moderate, responsible, and highly constructive leader. He was born on December 15, A.D. 37, in the small seaside town of An-

A bust of Nero, whose name has come to stand for the corruption of political power.

tium, about fifty miles south of Rome. His mother, Agrippina, great-granddaughter of Augustus, first married Nero's father, Gnaeus Domitius Ahenobarbus, an aristocrat with a reputation for shady dealings who died when the boy was three; later, in 49, Agrippina married the fourth emperor, Claudius, who himself was related by marriage to Augustus.[87] The

Agrippina, Nero's mother, was a scheming individual who tried to satisfy her own lust for power by promoting her son.

following year, when Nero was thirteen, Claudius adopted him as his son and soon after that named him as his successor.[88] This surprised many people because Claudius had a son of his own, Britannicus, three years Nero's junior; the reasons why Britannicus's father passed him over remain unclear; but it is likely that Agrippina, eager to promote Nero's interests, as well as her own, had much to do with it.

With her son now the heir apparent, the scheming and ambitious Agrippina grew increasingly impatient for her husband to die and finally took matters into her own hands. In October 54, she had Claudius poisoned and the sixteen-year-old Nero ascended the throne as Nero Claudius Caesar Augustus, fifth ruler of the Roman Empire. The accounts of Suetonius, Tacitus, Dio Cassius, and other ancient historians all agree that in his first months in power the new emperor tried hard to be generous and enlightened. As a guarantee of his virtuous intentions, Suetonius tells us, he gave a speech in the Senate, promising

> to model his rule on the principles laid down by Augustus, and never missed an opportunity of being generous or

merciful, or of showing how affable he was. He lowered, if he could not abolish, some of the heavier taxes. . . . If asked to sign the usual execution order for a felon, he would sigh: "Ah, how I wish that I had never learned to write!". . . . Once, when the Senate passed a vote of thanks to him, he answered: "Wait until I deserve them!" [89]

It is unclear how much of this early good behavior stemmed from Nero's own character and how much was the result of the influence of Lucius Annaeus Seneca, the brilliant philosopher-writer who had been the boy's tutor. On becoming one of the young emperor's two chief advisers, Seneca had penned both the conciliatory speech to the Senate and the moving oration Nero had delivered at Claudius's funeral. Evidence suggests that Seneca made a concerted effort to guide and restrain the youth, who, at least privately, must already have revealed signs of a neurotic, cruel, and violent nature. In his moral essay *On Mercy*, addressed directly to Nero, Seneca urged him to ask himself:

Have I of all mortals found favor with Heaven and been chosen to serve on earth as vicar for the gods? . . . I [should be able to say that I] have been moved neither by anger nor youthful impulse to unjust punishment. . . . With me the sword is hidden, nay, is sheathed; I am sparing to the utmost of even the meanest blood; no man fails to find favor at my hands. . . . Sternness I keep hidden, but mercy ever ready at hand. [90]

Several Royal Victims

Unfortunately for many Romans, eventually including Seneca himself, Nero did not live up to these sterling ideals. As the months and years passed, the young emperor's reign grew increasingly more brutal and despotic. First, he poisoned to death his stepbrother, thus eliminating any chance that a maturing Britannicus might try to challenge his position.

The next royal victim was Nero's mother, Agrippina. Though she had made his rise to power possible, he grew increasingly irritated with her criticisms and attempts to control him. In his masterful biography of Agrippina, scholar Anthony Barrett comments:

No matter how valuable Agrippina might be to Nero, it was almost inevitable that she would find it difficult to maintain her predominant position of influence and power. . . . Nero was a very young man, with an inflated opinion of his own talents and abilities, and it would have been natural for him to want to show that he was capable of establishing his own, independent role. . . . Nor did Agrippina's attitude help. . . . She tried to dictate his choice of friends, and . . . [he] was offended by her . . . constant criticism of his behavior. . . . A mother who constantly reminded him that he was an immature youth who needed to adhere to her advice . . . would soon wear out her welcome.[91]

Indeed, by March 59, Nero had had quite enough of Agrippina. He secretly ordered that a ship she was planning to board be rigged to sink; however, because she was a strong swimmer she made it safely to shore, and he ended up having to send soldiers to finish her off.

Nero's wives were no more immune to his nasty temper and cruelty. In 58, he became infatuated with Poppaea, the beautiful wife of his close friend Marcus Otho. The trouble was that the emperor was still married to Octavia, Claudius's daughter (whom Nero had wed in 53). In 62, Nero divorced Octavia, imprisoned her on a false charge of adultery, and then married Poppaea; however, the new royal couple evidently felt that poor Octavia had not suffered enough, for they had her killed and her head delivered to them. As it turned out, Poppaea did not gloat for long. The following year, after she had become pregnant, Nero threw a temper tantrum and kicked her to death.

A portrait of Nero, based on his likeness on a coin. One of his favorite pastimes was mugging unsuspecting people in the street.

Twisted Fantasies

Nero's relatives were not the only ones who suffered as his reign grew increasingly corrupt and violent. Once he had reduced taxes; now he raised them, as well as illegally confiscated the properties of several wealthy men, all to help finance his own excessive luxuries. He also derived perverse pleasure from disguising himself and mugging innocent strangers. "As soon as night fell," Suetonius writes,

he would snatch a cap or a wig and . . . prowl the streets in search of mischief. . . . One of his games was to attack men on their way home from dinner, stab them if they offered resistance, and then drop their bodies down the sewers. He would also break into shops and rob them. . . . During these escapades he often risked being blinded or killed—once he was beaten almost to death by a senator whose wife he had molested, which taught him never to go out after dark unless an escort of bodyguards was following him at an unobserved distance.[92]

Not surprisingly, as his misdeeds multiplied, the young emperor came to ignore Seneca and other responsible advisers, whose attempts to restrain him became less frequent and more delicate out of fear for their own well-being. From 62 on, Nero relied mainly on the advice of Ofonius Tigellinus, the ambitious commander of the Praetorian Guard, the elite military force charged with protecting the emperor. Tacitus claims that Tigellinus was an "intimate counselor of the emperor's brutalities";[93] and Plutarch goes so far as to call him "the very tutor and prompter of all the tyranny."[94] It is far too simple to lay all the blame on Tigellinus, however, and probably more accurate to say that he merely encouraged the expression of the negative traits the emperor already possessed.[95]

For instance, Tigellinus did not make Nero a flaming egotist who regularly indulged his twisted fantasies at the public's expense. Convinced that he was a divinely gifted singer, poet, and musician, the emperor performed in public and even entered contests, secretly bribing the judges to ensure he would win. He also fancied himself an actor. According to Suetonius, he played opposite professional actors, an activity then considered disgraceful for an upper-class person, let alone an emperor, "taking the parts of heroes and gods, sometimes even of heroines and goddesses, wearing masks either modeled on his own face, or on the face of whatever woman he happened to be in love with at the time."[96] Evidence suggests that his talents were mediocre at best; for example, Suetonius reports that his singing voice was "feeble and husky";[97] and spectators at his recitals, from which no one was allowed to leave, were so bored that some "feigned death and were carried away for burial."[98]

The Golden House

Nero's greatest notoriety, however, came in the wake of the terrible fire that devastated about two-thirds of the capital city in July 64. The blaze began in the wooden seats of the vast racing stadium, the Circus Maximus, and raged for nine days. Tacitus writes:

Breaking out in shops selling inflammable goods, and fanned by the wind, the conflagration instantly grew and swept . . . violently over the level spaces. Then it climbed the hills. . . . Of Rome's fourteen districts only four remained intact. Three were leveled to the ground. The other seven were reduced to a few scorched and mangled ruins.[99]

To his credit, Nero organized shelters for the homeless, launched ambitious rebuilding projects, and introduced a strict new building code that greatly reduced the risk of future fires.

But despite these commendable acts, many Romans became convinced that the emperor himself had purposely started the blaze, a charge that is almost certainly false.[100] Their suspicions stemmed from the use he made of a large area destroyed in the fire. Comprising nearly 350 acres of prime real estate in the heart of the city, this site had room for hundreds of new private and public buildings; however, the conceited and self-indulgent Nero decided to transform the entire area into his own personal pleasure park and palace. Under the direction of his talented architect, Severus, and chief engineer, Celer, what became known as the *Domus Aurea*, or Golden House, began to rise from the rubble.

This famous sculpture depicts members of the Praetorian Guard. Eventually, they, along with the senators, turned on Nero.

To many Romans, the Golden House seemed not only an unnecessary waste of money at a time when so many were in need, but also extremely out of place. The grandiose project was essentially a wealthy country villa set in the middle of the world's most crowded urban center. The living quarters alone covered some nine hundred thousand square feet, about 450 times the floor space of an average modern house. "The entrance-hall," writes Suetonius, "was large enough to contain a huge statue of himself, 120 feet high." [101] Outside this palatial residence stretched a vast parkland containing gardens, meadows, fishponds, game preserves, streams, waterfalls, and a pillar-lined, roofed walkway nearly a mile long. Suetonius gives these details of the emperor's "monument to himself":

An enormous pool, like a sea, was surrounded by buildings made to resemble cities, and by a landscape garden consisting of plowed fields, vineyards, pastures, and woodlands—where every variety of domestic and wild animal roamed about. Parts of the house were overlaid with gold [giving the place its name]. . . . All the dining-rooms had ceilings of . . . ivory, the panels of which could slide back and let a rain of flowers, or of perfume from hidden sprinklers, shower upon his guests. . . . When the palace had been decorated throughout in this lavish style, Nero dedicated it, and condescended to remark, "Good, now I can at last begin to live like a human being!" [102]

Poetic Justice

Many Romans came to see Nero's waste of valuable public space as a crime. In light of this and other offenses and outrages, several highly placed individuals, including senators and even some members of the Praetorian Guard, began to plot his assassination. To their regret, he discovered their schemes and attained revenge by torturing, executing, or exiling hundreds of people. Among these unfortunates was Seneca, whom Nero ordered to commit suicide.

The decadent emperor's own days turned out to be numbered, however. In March 68, worried that Nero's continued misrule might ruin the Empire, the governor of one of the Gallic provinces openly rebelled. Soon afterward, the troops of a military commander, Verginius Rufus, declared Rufus emperor; although Rufus refused the honor, Servius Galba, another provincial governor, accepted a similar acclamation from his own troops. Before long the Senate and Praetorian Guard recognized Galba's authority and Nero suddenly found himself in dire straits. He "woke at midnight," in Suetonius's words,

> to find that his bodyguard had deserted him. He leapt out of bed and summoned his friends. When they did not appear, he went . . . to their rooms. But all the doors were closed and no one answered. . . . "What? Have I then neither friends nor enemies left?" he cried, and dashed out of the palace. [103]

In the street, Nero met up with Phaon, one of his ex-slaves, who led him in disguise to a villa a few miles north of the city. There, the disgraced ruler spent some hours trying to work up the nerve to kill himself. "Dead! And so great an artist!" he supposedly wailed. Then a messenger arrived with a letter. "Nero tore it from the man's hands," Suetonius writes,

This modern drawing shows Nero just seconds after his suicide. Few, if any, Romans mourned his passing, since he had already killed the handful of people who had cared anything for him.

and read that, having been declared a public enemy by the Senate, he would be punished in the "ancient style" when arrested. He asked what "ancient style" meant, and learned that the executioners stripped their victim naked, thrust his head into a wooden fork, and then flogged him to death with rods.

This horrifying realization, coupled with the approach of soldiers coming to capture him, pushed him over the edge. He stabbed himself in the throat and "died, with eyes glazed and bulging from their sockets, a sight which horrified everybody present." [104]

Thus ended the reign of the then thirty-year-old Nero, one of the most infamous rulers of Rome or any other state. The date was June 9, 68, the sixth anniversary of his murder of his first wife, the innocent Octavia. Some of those who celebrated his death found some added satisfaction in observing that this coincidence contained a touch of poetic justice.

CHAPTER 8

Constantine: Soldier of Christ

The reign of Flavius Valerius Constantinus, known to history as Constantine I, "the Great," marked one of the major turning points in the Roman saga, and in European history as a whole. His significance lies chiefly in his steadfast support and promotion of Christianity, which up to his day had been a minor, hated, and often persecuted faith. It is certain that Christianity would not have spread so quickly, and indeed might never have triumphed, had it not been for Constantine. His granting its members toleration and economic and other privileges; his construction of churches and of Constantinople, the first truly Christian city; and his eventual conversion to the faith were key factors in its gaining social acceptance and new converts. Christianity subsequently exerted powerful religious and political authority in the Empire in its final years; and the faith went on to shape in profound and lasting ways the beliefs and events of the medieval and modern ages. For these reasons, Constantine fully deserves to be called one of the most influential and important rulers of Rome and of world history.

Father and Son

Constantine's rise to power was both dramatic and controversial. He was born in about 273 at Naissus in the province of Upper Moesia (now Nis in the nation of Serbia, north of Greece). He was very close to his mother, Helena, originally a barmaid, whom many years later, after her death, the Christian Church would declare a saint. His father, Constantius, was an outstanding professional soldier and close associate of Diocletian, who became emperor in 284. Thanks to Constantius's connections, Constantine grew up in the privileged, splendid, but sometimes volatile and dangerous atmosphere of the imperial court. That the boy would stand in line for positions of great power and influence was virtually assured when, in 293, at about twenty, his father was selected as Caesar, second in command to the western Augustus,

Maximian, in Diocletian's four-man ruling alliance, the Tetrarchy (Diocletian, the eastern Augustus, chose the military officer Galerius as his Caesar).

Dividing the Empire into four sections, each overseen by a powerful leader, was a bold experiment designed to make administering and defending the huge, far-flung realm more efficient. For his piece of the territorial pie, Constantius took charge of Gaul and Britain and ruled from Trier, near the Rhine River in what is now northern France. To ensure his allegiance and good behavior, the senior tetrarch, Diocletian, kept the youthful Constantine in the eastern capital of Nicomedia, in northern Asia Minor. This turned out to be unnecessary, however, for Constantius proved a loyal and effective ruler.

Constantine, whose toleration for Christianity helped to ensure that faith's survival.

When Diocletian retired in 305, he ordered Maximian, still the Augustus of the Empire's western half, to step down with him. The plan was for the two Caesars, Galerius and Constantius, to become the Augusti of a new tetrarchy. Nearly everyone expected Constantine, now an impressive, talented, and popular army officer in his early thirties, to be appointed Caesar to his father. According to the fourth-century Christian writer Lactantius:

> The gaze of all was upon Constantine. No one had any doubt; the soldiers who were present, the military officers . . . had eyes only for him; they were delighted with him . . . they were making their prayers for him. . . . A meeting of the troops was called . . . at which the old man [Diocletian] addressed them. . . . He was frail, he said, and was seeking rest after his labors; so he was handing over the imperial power to men who were more robust, and was appointing other Caesars in their place.[105]

To the surprise of most of those gathered, however, Constantine was passed over. Apparently, Galerius felt that the father-son combination of Constantius and Constantine would establish a western dynasty that might challenge his own power in the east.

Bowing to Galerius's wishes, therefore, Diocletian appointed Severus, a veteran army general, as Constantius's Caesar and Maximin (or Maximinus Daia), Galerius's young nephew, as Caesar to Galerius.

The Miraculous Vision

Soon after this turn of events, Constantine traveled to Gaul and from there crossed the English Channel into Britain to help his father deal with border raids by the Picts, a tribal people inhabiting what is now Scotland.[106] A few months later, on July 25, 306, at Eburacum (modern York), Constantius, who had been ill for some time, died. His troops enthusiastically proclaimed Constantine the new western Augustus; but Galerius refused to allow this promotion to stand and demoted Constantine to the rank of Caesar while elevating Severus above him to the position of Augustus. Reasoning that he was not yet powerful enough to dispute this arrangement, for the time being Constantine accepted it.

In the following year, however, Constantine did attain the title of Augustus, as the result of the outbreak of a full-fledged civil war among the tetrarchs and some ambitious usurpers. First, Maxentius, son of the retired tetrarch Maximian, seized the city of Rome and illegally declared himself emperor. The father joined the son and pushed Severus aside, and then, hoping to secure Constantine's support, Maximian offered to make Constantine an Augustus. Constantine accepted and married Maximian's daughter, Fausta, to seal the bargain. Complicating matters, in 308, Maximian and Maxentius had a falling-out and the father fled to Gaul and joined his son-in-law against his own son; but two years later, Maximian switched sides again, tried unsuccessfully to defeat Constantine, and died shortly thereafter.

The climax of the civil war came in 312, as Constantine marched his army into Italy, intent on unseating Maxentius. According to Constantine's contemporary biographer, the Christian bishop Eusebius, on October 27, as the army neared Rome, Constantine beheld a miraculous vision:

> He saw with his own eyes the trophy of a cross of light in the heavens, above the sun, and an inscription, "CONQUER BY THIS," attached to it. At this sight he himself was struck with amazement. . . . And while he continued to ponder and reason on its meaning, night overtook him; then in his sleep the Christ of God appeared to him . . . and commanded him to make a like of that sign which he had seen

in the heavens, and to use it as a safeguard in all engagements with his enemies.[107]

The reality of these visions, which Eusebius wrote about many years later, remains debatable.[108] What is more certain is that the next day, Constantine had his soldiers paint onto their shields a Christian symbol (composed of chi and rho, the first two letters of the Greek version of Christ's name). Then, at Rome's Milvian Bridge, the two armies clashed and Constantine won a stunning

One of the many later representations of Constantine's famous miraculous vision. The celestial inscription translates "Conquer by this."

victory, sending Maxentius and several thousand of his men to watery graves in the Tiber.

Repaying the Deity

Constantine's apparently Christian-aided victory seems satisfactorily to explain the favor and support he showed the Christians thereafter. Like nearly all other people of his day, he was both deeply religious and highly superstitious; and he could be expected not only to attribute his win to the Christian god, but also handsomely to repay that deity by helping its followers. It must be emphasized that Constantine did not actually convert to the faith at this moment. For a long time he remained a pagan, or non-Christian, who accepted the existence of and showed favor and gratitude to the Christian god. It was not unusual for Roman rulers to pay homage to multiple gods, and Constantine continued to do so for many years.

At first, Constantine's support for the faith must have perplexed many of his pagan subjects, for the Christians were at the time still few in number and generally detested. For generations, the Christians had been viewed with suspicion, hatred, and even disgust. They refused to worship the state gods, insisting on the supremacy of their own god, and were suspected, wrongly it turned out, of horrible crimes, including child murder and incest. So a number of Roman leaders, beginning with Nero, persecuted them over the faith's first three centuries of existence.[109] The worst of these persecutions, including the burning of churches, destruction of holy books, and torture and execution of many of the faithful, was launched in the east in 303 by Galerius, a vehement anti-Christian.

In the western part of the realm, by contrast, Maximian and Constantius were much more lenient with the Christians. For example, Constantius closed some churches but took no further action. And when Constantine succeeded his father in 306, he pursued an even more humane policy, granting the Christians in the provinces he controlled complete toleration. This at least partly explains why he so readily adopted their symbol and called on their god to help him attain victory at the Milvian Bridge. Afterward, to reward them, he showed them increasing support.

The first and perhaps most momentous demonstration of that support was a decree of toleration for all Christians in the Empire. Constantine, now undisputed master of the western Roman sphere, went to Milan, in northern Italy, in February 313, to meet with Valerius Licinius, master of the eastern sphere (Licinius had earlier been appointed Augustus by Galerius, who had died in

311). The two emperors agreed on the toleration decree and Licinius later issued what became known as the Edict of Milan in both their names.[110] "When under happy auspices," it began,

> I, Constantine Augustus, and I, Licinius Augustus, had come to Milan and held an inquiry about all matters such as pertain to the common advantage and good . . . we resolved to issue decrees by which esteem and reverence for the Deity might be procured, that is, that we might give all Christians freedom of choice to follow the ritual which they wished.[111]

Energy, Intelligence, and Tirelessness

Despite the good relations the Augusti established at Milan, their alliance rapidly deteriorated. Disputes over succession and territorial borders led to open warfare in 316; soon afterward Licinius unexpectedly violated the toleration decree by launching an anti-Christian persecution, giving Constantine additional motivation to oppose him. The final showdown took place at Adrianople, in northern Greece, on July 3, 324. Licinius went down to defeat and for the next thirteen years Constantine reigned as sole emperor, the first man to rule both western and eastern Rome since Diocletian had first divided the leadership in 286.

This idealized portrait of Constantine emphasizes his piety. But he could be ruthless as well.

Both during these power struggles and throughout the rest of his reign, Constantine's fascination and support for Christianity remained steadfast. He granted its clergy, led by the bishops, government subsidies. And he invited leading bishops to attend him at the imperial court, where they joined the impressive retinue of nobles, scribes, clerks, and other officials that always surrounded him when he appeared in public. These bishops eventually assumed such a prominent role in Constantine's life that Eusebius compared their relationship to that of Christ and his apostles.

Constantine also acted as mediator of several serious disputes that arose among the bishops. Now that Christianity was considered a legitimate religion, it was only natural that he would assume such a role, since the Roman emperors traditionally considered it their duty to oversee religion and thereby secure the favor of the gods for the benefit of the Empire. The most famous of his Christian mediations was the council held in 325 at Nicaea, not far south of Nicomedia. More than two hundred bishops attended this first of the seven so-called Ecumenical Councils held over the course of the next four centuries, meetings that established much important church doctrine.

During these crucial formative years, the Christian Church was fortunate to have a figure of such vitality and authority fighting for it. Indeed, to his religious, military, and political endeavors alike, Constantine brought extraordinary levels of energy, intelligence, and sheer force of will; it was said that his imposing appearance in his impressive battle array or court finery elicited feelings of awe and respect from both Christians and pagans. About his physical attributes, Eusebius wrote, "No one was comparable to him for grace and beauty of person, or height of stature; and he so far surpassed his peers in personal strength as to be a terror to them." [112] And about his forceful, compelling character, the great Edward Gibbon remarked:

> In the dispatch of business, his diligence was indefatigable [tireless]; and the active powers of his mind were almost continually exercised in reading, writing, or meditating, in giving audience to ambassadors, and in examining the complaints of his subjects. Even [his opponents] were compelled to acknowledge that he possessed . . . [the] patience to execute the most arduous designs [goals]. . . . In the field, he infused his own intrepid spirit into the troops, whom he conducted with the talents of a consummate general. . . . The boundless ambition, which, from the moment of accepting the purple at York [in 306], appears as the ruling passion of his soul, may be justified by the dangers of his situation . . . [and] by the prospect that his success would enable him to restore peace and order to the distracted Empire. [113]

A Prodigious Builder

Both Christianity and the Empire as a whole also benefited from Constantine's prodigious building programs, particularly his founding of Constantinople in 330. His principal aim was to establish a strong base from which to defend the Empire's eastern

A dramatic representation of Constantine bestowing on the city of Byzantium the new name of Constantinople, as a mason carves the founding stone.

sphere against attacks from the north and east. The city's location, on the Bosporus (the site of the Greek town of Byzantium), was a strategically strong position for the command and defense of Greece and the Balkans in the west, Asia Minor in the east, and the Black and Aegean Seas. Because of the emperor's support of the Christians and their increasing power and influence, Constantinople also grew into a mighty Christian bastion.

The modern version of St. Peter's Basilica stands on the same site as the original, built by order of Constantine.

Constantine also erected numerous Christian churches, not only in Constantinople but in other important cities across the Empire. Among the largest were those in his former Gallic capital of Trier and in Rome, where work began on the original version of St. Peter's Basilica in about 332. In fact, the basilica, a traditional Roman building form, became the standard pattern for most of these early churches. Michael Grant explains:

> These basilicas were oblong buildings, containing . . . side-aisles, divided off from the central nave by arched colonnades [rows of columns]. . . . These splendid churches, which set such a stamp on the future, owed a great many . . . features to the pagan basilicas of the past, which had served at one and the same time as market, meeting-place, and law court. . . . The interiors of the churches as a whole were spacious, dignified, and designed to encourage spiritual elevation.[114]

Constantine had more grand architectural and administrative plans for his vast realm than he would live to carry out. Shortly before Easter in 337, he became seriously ill and, feeling that death was near, asked to be baptized.[115] Eusebius, bishop of Nicomedia (not the emperor's biographer of the same name), performed the ceremony, shortly after which the emperor died. His body was laid in a golden coffin covered with purple draperies and placed in the central hall of his palace at Constantinople, where tens of thousands of his grieving subjects filed by to pay their last respects. Doubtless the saddest among them were Christians, who were (and remain today) deeply in his debt. To them, he was more than a mere emperor; he was first and foremost a soldier of Christ; and indeed, that has been the judgment of posterity.

CHAPTER 9

Justinian: Preserver of Rome's Legacy

Justinian, who ruled the eastern Roman realm from his capital of Constantinople from 527 to 565, is often referred to by historians as the last true Roman emperor (his many successors to the throne of that realm, until its fall in 1453, are usually termed Byzantine rulers). After the fall of the western Roman sphere to the Goths and other barbarians in the late fifth century, the eastern emperors felt that they were the rightful rulers of the lost western lands. Constantinople was at the time, and remained for many centuries afterward, Michael Grant points out, "the largest and most splendid and most learned city in Europe." And although its culture and language were predominately Greek, and its art was a blend of Roman, Greek, and Oriental elements, "its emperors saw themselves as the heirs of ancient Rome and called themselves 'Kings of the Romans.'" [116]

The dream of reuniting east and west and of restoring the Roman Empire to it past glories culminated in Justinian's large-scale military conquests of northern Africa and Italy. Ultimately, these efforts proved futile and the dream died with him. Yet during his long and tumultuous reign, he managed to organize and publish the massive collection of laws that constitutes one of Roman civilization's two or three greatest achievements. This accomplishment, which preserved a legacy that profoundly shaped the course of later European culture, ranks Justinian as one of the pivotal rulers of Western history.

From Peasant to Politician

Justinian was born Petrus Sabbatius at Tauresium, a village near Naissus, Constantine the Great's native town, in about 482, some six years after the last western emperor was forced from the throne. Though of peasant birth, young Petrus had a family connection to the government, namely his uncle, Justin, a successful army officer who had gained influence at court. Justin brought the boy to the capital and saw to it that he received the best Latin and Greek education then available. When Justin became emperor in 518, he made Petrus, then a capable and enterprising politician in his thirties, one of his chief personal advisers; increasingly the aging ruler came to rely on his nephew to make important administrative decisions. Eventually, the emperor adopted the younger man as his son and heir. Petrus thereby became Flavius Petrus Sabbatius Justinianus, known more simply as Justinian.

In 521, Justinian served as consul. Much changed from the powerful office of late republican times, a consul in this period was mainly charged with appeasing the masses by staging chariot races and other games in the capital's large amphitheater, the Hippodrome. He came openly to support the Blues, one of the two most influential racing factions, against their rivals, the Greens. These factions, historian Robert Browning explains,

Justinian, who had grand dreams of reuniting the eastern and western spheres of the Roman Empire.

> were able to whip up a crowd or empty the streets at will
> . . . [and] enjoyed from their supporters the fanatical loy-
> alty which some football teams arouse today. In a city in
> which there were no political parties and no elections, they
> served as safety-valves for popular discontent and as a
> means of pressure upon the authorities. A man who aimed
> at power had much to gain from their support.[117]

Justinian took full advantage of the support he received from the Blues. Gangs of Blues roamed the streets, enforcing his and their own will on the populace; at least that is the way Justinian's contemporary, the sixth-century historian Procopius, told it:

> At first they were destroying their rival partisans, but as time
> went on they began to slay also those who had given them
> no offense at all. . . . And these things took place no longer
> in darkness or concealment, but at all hours of the day . . .
> for the wrongdoers had no need to conceal their crimes, for
> no dread of punishment lay on them. . . . And thereby he
> [Justinian] brought the Roman state to its knees.[118]

Roman charioteers tear around the track of Constantinople's Hippodrome. Popular racing factions were instrumental in Justinian's rise to power.

It must be emphasized that Procopius, our chief source for this period, was a hostile witness. Secretary to the brilliant military general Belisarius, the historian, for reasons that remain unclear, developed a hatred for Justinian. His attacks on Justinian in his notorious *Secret History*, even if sometimes based in fact, are certainly one-sided and at times highly exaggerated or false. One prominent historian calls the work "the angry retaliation of a disappointed courtier." [119]

Securing the Throne

Procopius was especially hard on Theodora, whom Justinian met and fell desperately in love with in the early 520s. The daughter of a bear trainer at the Hippodrome, she worked as an actress and a stripper; these professions were considered so lowly and unseemly that a law forbade those who practiced them from marrying an upper-class person. According to Procopius, Theodora was also a disreputable prostitute and wanton pleasure seeker who had frequent and scandalous sexual escapades. "The girl had not a particle of modesty," he claimed, "nor did any man ever see her embarrassed, but she undertook shameless services without the least hesitation." [120] It is possible that, like many actresses in her day, Theodora at one time supplemented her income through prostitution. But balancing Procopius's denunciations of her was her later steadfast love and devotion for Justinian. In 525 the emperor, obviously at his nephew's urgings, changed the law, thus allowing Justinian and Theodora to marry; thereafter she proved a loyal, courageous, level-headed, and dignified partner and adviser to her husband. Theirs remains one of the great love stories of history.

Theodora certainly played a major role in resolving the first major crisis Justinian faced after ascending the throne at Justin's death in 527. By 532, sporadic violence between the Blue and Green racing factions had so escalated as to force the government to arrest several faction leaders. This action touched off a citywide riot that almost destroyed the capital. The magnificent church of St. Sophia, part of the imperial palace, and other buildings were burned as angry crowds rampaged, screaming *"Nika!"* or "Victory!," the name by which the rebellion came to be known. In defiance of the government, the rebels proclaimed a senator as emperor and crowded into the Hippodrome to watch him take the imperial seat. Meanwhile, Justinian considered fleeing; however, Theodora forcefully argued that he stay and fight for the throne. Drawing strength from her bravery and resolution, he unleashed the capable Belisarius, whose troops immediately entered the Hippodrome and slaughtered more than thirty thousand people.

After this decisive event, Justinian's throne was secure. But his harsh response to the riots, combined with his later initiation of

In this mosaic, Justinian's wife, Theodora, holds a golden chalice intended as a gift for a church, the dome of which hovers above her head.

costly wars and heavy taxation, made him generally unpopular with the majority of his subjects. Still, some admired him for his dedication to duty, hard work, and willingness to listen to all petitioners. In one of the *Secret History*'s few moments of praise, Procopius spoke of his "easy-going disposition" and called him "the most accessible person in the world. For even men of low estate and altogether obscure had complete freedom . . . to come before . . . and to converse with him." [121] Justinian also won praise for his rebuilding of the ruined St. Sophia. "Disregarding all questions of expense," Procopius said,

> [the emperor] eagerly [began] the work of construction, and [gathered] all the [best] artisans from the whole world. . . . So the church has become a spectacle of marvelous beauty, overwhelming to those who see it . . . for it soars to a height to match the sky, and as if surging up from amongst the other buildings it stands on high and looks down upon the remainder of the city, adorning it. [122]

The Civilizing Force of Law

As grand a project as St. Sophia's restoration was, Justinian surpassed it in the two main undertakings of his reign. The first was his great codification of Roman laws. Justinian strongly believed that law was the most important force holding civilized society together and, like other Roman leaders, was proud of Rome's impressive legal heritage. However, by his day the books, imperial edicts, and opinions of distinguished jurists making up that heritage had grown into an enormous, confusing mass of material. Over the centuries Rome had produced so many laws that no law school, let alone a single individual, could hope to collect and read them all in a lifetime. Moreover, many laws were hopelessly out of date or written for a pagan rather than a Christian society. Three previous attempts had been made to sift through and codify this mess: two, by the lawyers Gregorius and Hermogenes, in Diocletian's reign (late 290s), and another during the reign of Theodosius II (late 430s); but all these were small in scale and had become dated and useless by the sixth century.

Early in 528, Justinian gave a skilled and energetic lawyer named Tribonian the awesome task of producing an up-to-date, usable compilation of Roman laws. The emperor outlined his ambitious goal in an edict issued in February of that year:

> What many emperors saw needed rectifying, but none has ventured to put into effect, we have decided to grant now to

Justinian (center) stands with soldiers and priests. His monumental codification of Roman laws was perhaps his greatest single accomplishment.

the world, with the help of Almighty God, and to . . . [prune] the multitude of enactments contained in the three codes of Gregorius, Hermogenes, and Theodosius . . . by compiling a single Code which shall bear our own name, and shall contain the enactments of the above-mentioned codes and the new laws promulgated [enacted] after them.[123]

Considering the great size and complexity of the job, Tribonian and his staff of lawyers, clerks, and copyists worked with incredible speed; the *Codex Justinianus*, or *Justinian Code*, was issued on April 7, 529, and thereafter only the laws contained within it could be cited in the courts.

The next step was to compile and edit the immense accumulation of jurists' opinions about the meaning and interpretation of these laws. Faced with a volume of material totaling over 3 million lines, Tribonian and his staff went to work in December 530. Almost exactly three years later, the completed work, known as the *Digest*, consisting of about 150,000 lines, was published. The opinions cited in the *Digest* now had the force of law and constituted the exclusive and standard interpretation of the legal statutes in the *Code*. About the lasting impact of the work as a whole, the noted historian Will Durant remarks:

For some generations [it] gave order and security to a motley assemblage of peoples, and allowed, across the fron-

Vandal warriors march toward Rome. The Vandals held firm control of northern Africa until Justinian's troops defeated them.

tiers and along the streets of a dozen nations, freer and safer movement than the same regions enjoy today. It continued to the end the code of the Byzantine Empire; and five centuries after it disappeared in the West it was revived by the jurists of Italy, accepted by emperors and popes, and entered like a scaffolding of order into the structure of many modern states.[124]

Reconquest of the West

The same year that the *Digest* appeared, Justinian initiated the largest single undertaking of his reign—the reconquest of the western Roman lands lost to the barbarians in the preceding two generations. Fearing that expeditions sent so far away against reportedly fearsome, entrenched enemies would end in disaster, Justinian's generals opposed his plans. But he insisted that victory could be achieved and his confidence proved, at least in the short run, to be well founded.

The first target was northern Africa, then in the possession of the fierce Vandals, who had sacked Rome in 455. In June 533, Belisarius departed at the head of an armada of 92 warships and some 500 transport vessels, carrying about 15,000 infantry and 5,000 cavalry (along with about 30,000 sailors). The fleet first landed in Sicily. There, Belisarius's assistant, the historian Procopius, discovered from a trader who had recently been to Carthage that the Vandals had no knowledge of their approach. Swiftly taking advantage of the element of surprise, the Romans landed unopposed about 150 miles south of Carthage; and not long afterward, they met and crushed the Vandal army. According to Procopius's eyewitness account:

> The battle became fierce, and many of the noblest of the Vandals fell. . . . Then at last the whole Roman army was set in motion, and crossing the river they advanced upon the enemy, and the rout, beginning at the center, became complete; for each of the Roman divisions turned to flight those before them with no trouble . . . and they pursued the fugitives throughout the whole night, killing all the men . . . and making slaves of the women and children.[125]

In the following year, Belisarius invaded Italy, then held by the Ostrogoths. There the Romans had a more difficult time, partly because their army was smaller than the one that had captured Africa. Also, the Ostrogoths were more resilient than the Vandals, and the local Italian population was not all that enthusiastic about being rescued by Greek-speaking strangers. For these reasons, the war dragged on for some twenty years before another of Justinian's generals, Narses, managed to reconquer Rome and most of the rest of Italy.

Widespread Poverty and Misery

In the end, these costly efforts did not achieve Justinian's long-range goal of creating a new Mediterranean-wide Roman Empire. Although parts of the west remained under Byzantine control for some time to come, most remained in a desolate state and became a drain on eastern resources. The sad fact was that, through constant warfare and neglect, most of Italy had by now lost most vestiges of civil and social organization; the city of Rome's population had shrunk from its fourth-century level of perhaps eight hundred thousand to twenty-five thousand at most; and poverty and misery were rampant. Facing these hard realities was Justinian, now an old man who lacked both the will and the huge financial resources that would have been needed to rebuild, revitalize, and defend the reclaimed regions.

During the years of the conquests, several factors had taken their toll on Justinian's imperial and personal resources. Of the two most noteworthy, the first was the dreaded bubonic plague, which in 542 began to ravage the Mediterranean world. Particularly serious outbreaks of the disease crippled Constantinople in 543 and 558; it is estimated that as many as three hundred thousand people, perhaps 40 percent of the city's population, died in the first outbreak alone. The emperor himself contracted it, although he recovered in a weakened state. Undoubtedly more debilitating to Justinian, in 548 his beloved Theodora died, probably of cancer. None of the writers of the period described his specific reaction to this loss, but from what is known about the extraordinary closeness of this royal couple, he must have been devastated.

The victorious Belisarius kneels before Justinian after the general's successful capture of the African Vandal kingdom.

Byzantine Empire Under Justinian I (A.D. 527–565)

Justinian himself died on November 14, 565, presumably of a heart attack or stroke. His body, resting on a golden bier studded with jewels, was carried through the streets while his successor, his nephew Justin, and a procession of state officials, bishops, priests, and soldiers marched behind. They placed Justinian beside Theodora in the royal tomb while the clergy said a mass and offered prayers for the couple's souls. None then present could have known that they were marking the end of an age. As the noted Byzantine scholar John J. Norwich puts it:

> Far from inaugurating the glorious new era of which he had dreamt, Justinian was the last Roman emperor to occupy the throne of Byzantium. It was not simply that he had been born a Latin. . . . It was that his mind was cast in a Latin mold, and that throughout his reign he devoted the greater part of his prodigious energies to the restoration of the old Roman Empire. What he never understood was that that Empire was by now [outmoded]; the days when one man could stand in undisputed universal authority were gone and would not return.[126]

Yet though he never achieved his grandest goal in the literal sense, Justinian helped to ensure ancient Rome's intellectual and spiritual survival. Having inherited the accumulated wealth of centuries of Roman culture and law, he managed to preserve a substantial portion of it for future generations; and in the form of that remarkable legacy, which has in diverse ways made the world what it is, in a very real sense Rome still lives.

NOTES

Chapter 1: A Brief History of Ancient Rome

1. The traditional view was that these tribal peoples migrated in waves across the Alps; however, studies of the distribution of early Italian languages have led a number of scholars to conclude that at least some early migrants moved southwestward through the Balkans and crossed the Adriatic Sea into eastern Italy.

2. For an explanation of how these scholars arrived at this date, see T. J. Cornell, *The Beginnings of Rome: Italy and Rome from the Bronze Age to the Punic Wars (c.1000–264 B.C.)*. London: Routledge, 1995, pp. 72–73.

3. Livy, *The History of Rome from Its Foundation* 1.6, 8–9. Books 1–5 published as *Livy: The Early History of Rome*. Translated by Aubrey de Sélincourt. New York: Penguin Books, 1971, pp. 40, 42–43.

4. Cornell, *The Beginnings of Rome*, p. 60.

5. Cicero, *For Cluentius* 53.146, in *Cicero: Murder Trials*. Translated by Michael Grant. New York: Penguin Books, 1990, pp. 216–17.

6. Some cities and districts were less receptive to being Romanized than others. A few Etruscan towns, for instance, retained many of their old ways, including their native language (spoken by many of them alongside Latin), until as late as the first century B.C. By that time, the Romans looked on them as quaint, backward, and in some ways even barbaric.

7. Michael Grant, *History of Rome*. New York: Scribner's, 1978, pp. 65–66.

8. The term *Punic* was derived from the Latin word *Punicus*, meaning Phoenician, the name of the Near Eastern maritime people who founded Carthage in about 850 B.C.

9. Polybius, *The Histories* 1.20, published as *Polybius: The Rise of the Roman Empire*. Translated by Ian Scott-Kilvert. New York: Penguin Books, 1979, p. 62.

10. F. R. Cowell, *Cicero and the Roman Republic*. Baltimore: Penguin Books, 1967, p. 209.

11. A. H. M. Jones, *Augustus*. New York: W. W. Norton, 1970, p. 7.

12. Edward Gibbon, *The Decline and Fall of the Roman Empire*. 3 vols. Edited by David Womersley. New York: Penguin Books, 1994, vol. 1, pp. 101–103.

13. Arthur E. R. Boak, *A History of Rome to 565 A.D.* New York: Macmillan, 1943, pp. 455–56. The rich Roman landlords and their dependent tenants formed part of the basis for the manorial system of lords and serfs that later became widespread in medieval Europe.

14. To that effect, Diocletian issued an economic edict in 301; but the move was extremely unpopular because people did not like the government telling them what they could earn or charge for goods, and the policy ultimately failed. For a translation of the edict, including its lengthy list of proposed prices, see Naphtali Lewis and Meyer Reinhold, eds., *Roman Civilization: Sourcebook II: The Empire*. New York: Harper and Row, 1966, pp. 463–73.

15. Averil Cameron, *The Later Roman Empire: A.D. 284–430*. Cambridge, MA: Harvard University Press, 1993, p. 39.

16. Jerome, Letter 127, quoted in John J. Norwich, *Byzantium: The Early Centuries*. New York: Knopf, 1989, p. 119; also see F. H. Wright's translation for the Loeb Classical Library, *Select Letters of St. Jerome*. Cambridge, MA: Harvard University Press, 1963, p. 463.

17. Solomon Katz, *The Decline of Rome and the Rise of Medieval Europe*. Ithaca, NY: Cornell University Press, 1955, p. 139.

Chapter 2: Fabius: Shield of the Roman People

18. By modern standards, Roman humor was often blunt, graphic, personal, and even cruel; one common example, especially in early Roman times, was to assign both children and adults unflattering nicknames, such as "lame," "stammerer," "fat," "onion," and "pig"; hence the name Cicero was derived from the word for "chickpea," and Fabius was called "wart-covered."

19. Plutarch, *Life of Fabius* 1, in *Makers of Rome: Nine Lives by Plutarch*. Translated by Ian Scott-Kilvert. New York: Penguin Books, 1965, pp. 53–54.

20. According to Livy, the Saguntine men "in desperation either fought to the death or set fire to their own houses and burned themselves alive together with their wives and children." (*The History of Rome from Its Foundation* 21.24. Books 21–30 pub-

lished as *Livy: The War with Hannibal*. Translated by Aubrey de Sélincourt. New York: Penguin Books, 1972, p. 38.)

21. Livy, 21.18, in *War With Hannibal*, pp. 41–42.

22. Plutarch, *Fabius* 3, in *Makers of Rome*, pp. 55–56.

23. Plutarch, *Fabius* 5, in *Makers of Rome*, p. 58.

24. Livy, 22.23, in *War with Hannibal*, p. 120.

25. Quoted in Livy, 22.14, in *War with Hannibal*, pp. 109, 111.

26. Quoted in Plutarch, *Fabius* 12, in *Makers of Rome*, p. 67.

27. Quoted in Plutarch, *Fabius* 13, in *Makers of Rome*, p. 68.

28. By this time, Hannibal, who had first reached Italy with only about twenty-six thousand men, had been reinforced by Gauls and other Roman inhabitants of northern Italy who still held grudges against Rome for its past aggressions against them.

29. Polybius, 3.115–16, in *Rise of the Roman Empire*, pp. 271–273.

30. Plutarch, *Fabius* 17, in *Makers of Rome*, pp. 72–73.

31. Plutarch, *Fabius* 27, in *Makers of Rome*, p. 83.

Chapter 3: Marius: First of the Military Strongmen

32. Sallust, *The Jugurthine War* 63, in *Sallust: The Jugurthine War/The Conspiracy of Catiline*. Translated by S. A. Handford. New York: Penguin Books, 1988, pp. 99–100.

33. Quoted in Sallust, *Jugurthine War* 85, in Handford translation, p. 117.

34. Plutarch, *Life of Marius* 3, in *Fall of the Roman Republic: Six Lives by Plutarch*. Translated by Rex Warner. New York: Penguin Books, 1972, p. 15.

35. Sallust, *Jugurthine War* 63, in Handford translation, p. 99. The rank of military tribune, or "tribal officer," was a prestigious one. Each legion (a regiment of four to six thousand men, depending on type and period) was commanded by six tribunes, some of whom were elected by the Assembly and others chosen by the consuls who led the armies. See Lawrence Keppie, *The Making of the Roman Army*. New York: Barnes and Noble, 1994, pp. 14, 39–40.

36. Quoted in Plutarch, *Marius* 6, in *Fall of the Roman Republic*, p. 18.

37. Plutarch, *Marius* 10, in *Fall of the Roman Republic*, p. 22.

38. Phillip A. Kildahl, *Caius Marius*. New York: Twayne, 1968, p. 65.

39. Grant, *History of Rome*, p. 180.

40. Plutarch, *Marius* 13, in *Fall of the Roman Republic*, p. 25.

41. Plutarch, *Marius* 11, in *Fall of the Roman Republic*, p. 24.

42. Plutarch, *Marius* 21, in *Fall of the Roman Republic*, p. 34.

43. Plutarch, *Marius* 45, in *Fall of the Roman Republic*, p. 61.

Chapter 4: Caesar: Politician, Conqueror, and Dictator

44. Plutarch, *Life of Sulla* 31, in *Fall of the Roman Republic*, p. 105.

45. Quoted in Suetonius, *Life of Caesar* 1, in *Lives of the Twelve Caesars*, published as *The Twelve Caesars*. Translated by Robert Graves and revised by Michael Grant. New York: Penguin Books, 1979, p. 14.

46. Suetonius, *Caesar* 45, in *Twelve Caesars*, p. 34.

47. Plutarch, *Life of Caesar* 4, in *Fall of the Roman Republic*, p. 246.

48. Matthias Gelzer, *Caesar: Politician and Statesman*. Cambridge, MA: Harvard University Press, 1968, p. 332.

49. Quaestors were elected by the Assembly for one-year terms. The job entailed maintaining public records, overseeing the treasury, and acting as paymaster for generals on campaigns and as secretaries to governors.

50. Quoted in Sallust, *The War with Catiline* 51, in *Works*. Translated by J. C. Rolfe. New York: Cambridge University Press, 1965, pp. 91, 99.

51. Julius Caesar, *Commentary on the Gallic War* 1.1, in *War Commentaries of Caesar*. Translated by Rex Warner. New York: New American Library, 1960, p. 11.

52. Suetonius, *Caesar* 57, in *Twelve Caesars*, p. 40.

53. Quoted in Suetonius, *Caesar* 32, in *Twelve Caesars*, p. 28.

54. Caesar significantly reduced unemployment by establishing new colonies in Greece, Spain, and northern Africa, to which over eighty thousand jobless Romans immediately immigrated. He also tried to fight crime by increasing the severity of criminal penalties; proposed a law (which, owing to his death, was never passed) intended to reduce significantly the number of slaves in Rome (then constituting perhaps one-third of the population); began planning the construction of enormous new canals in

Italy and Greece; and, with the aid of the Greek astronomer Sosigenes, introduced a new, more accurate calendar of 365 days, which served as the basis for the modern Western version.

55. Christian Meier, *Caesar*. Translated by David McLintock. New York: HarperCollins, 1996, p. 481.

Chapter 5: Cicero: Last Champion of the Republic

56. Letter 2.6, April 59 B.C., in Cicero, *Letters to Atticus*. 3 vols. Translated by E. O. Winstedt. Cambridge, MA: Harvard University Press, 1961, vol. 1, pp. 125-27.

57. John C. Rolfe, *Cicero and His Influence*. New York: Cooper Square, 1963, p. 63.

58. Plutarch, *Life of Cicero* 1, in *Fall of the Roman Republic*, p. 312.

59. Plutarch, *Cicero* 5, in *Fall of the Roman Republic*, pp. 315-16.

60. Cicero, *First Oration Against Verres* 1, 15, in *Cicero: Selected Works*. Translated by Michael Grant. New York: Penguin Books, 1971, pp. 37, 54.

61. After Cicero finished his long denunciation of Verres, the latter, instead of waiting for the next stage of the trial, conceded guilt by going into voluntary exile and paying a huge monetary fine. Cicero later published the speech, along with five others he had prepared but not had the chance to deliver. The standard modern translation of all six speeches is *Verrine Orations*. 2 vols. Translated by L. H. G. Greenwood. Cambridge, MA: Harvard University Press, 1966.

62. Cicero, *On Duties* 1.72-73, in *De Officiis*. Translated by Walter Miller. Cambridge, MA: Harvard University Press, 1961, p. 75.

63. Cicero, *First Speech Against Catiline* 1.1, in *Selected Political Speeches of Cicero*. Translated by Michael Grant. Baltimore: Penguin Books, 1979, p. 76.

64. Sallust, *Conspiracy of Catiline* 32, in Handford translation, pp. 198-99.

65. Sallust, *Conspiracy of Catiline* 55, in Handford translation, p. 227.

66. Plutarch, *Cicero* 32, in *Fall of the Roman Republic*, p. 343.

67. After forcing Cicero into exile, Clodius burned down his houses and tried to sell his lands, but, out of respect for Cicero, no one expressed an interest. The Senate soon declared that unless Cicero was allowed to return, it would no longer ratify legisla-

tion. Later, after Pompey used his triumviral power to suppress Clodius and Cicero returned to Rome, the government rebuilt the orator's ruined homes at public expense.

68. Letter 8.13, March 1, 49 B.C., in Cicero, *Letters to Atticus*, vol. 2, pp. 161–63.

69. Cicero himself called them Philippics as a joke, in reference to the fourth-century B.C. Athenian orator Demosthenes' famous series of verbal attacks on Macedonia's aggressive king, Philip II.

70. Cicero, *First Philippic Against Marcus Antonius* 14, in *Selected Political Speeches of Cicero*, p. 316.

71. Cicero, *Second Philippic Against Marcus Antonius*, 2, 3, 18, 45, in *Cicero: Selected Works*, pp. 104–105, 122, 152.

72. Plutarch, *Cicero* 48, in *Fall of the Roman Republic*, p. 360.

73. Cicero, *On Duties* 3.21, in *Cicero: Selected Works*, p. 191.

74. Torsten Petersson, *Cicero: A Biography*. New York: Biblo and Tannen, 1963, p. 685.

Chapter 6: Augustus: Architect of the Empire

75. Suetonius, *Life of Augustus* 80–81, in *Twelve Caesars*, pp. 98–99.

76. Henry T. Rowell, *Rome in the Augustan Age*. Norman: University of Oklahoma Press, 1962, pp. 16–17.

77. Letter 14.12, April 22, 44 B.C., in Cicero, *Letters to Atticus*, vol. 3, p. 241.

78. Plutarch, *Life of Antony* 16, in *Fall of the Roman Republic*, p. 16.

79. Augustus, *Res gestae*, in Paul J. Alexander, ed., *The Ancient World: To 300 A.D.* New York: Macmillan, 1963, p. 263.

80. Appian, *Civil Wars* 4.2–3, in *Appian: The Civil Wars*. Translated by John Carter. New York: Penguin Books, 1996, pp. 209–10.

81. Virgil, *Georgics*, quoted in Gilbert Charles-Picard, *Augustus and Nero: The Secret of Empire*. Translated by Len Ortzen. New York: Thomas Y. Crowell, 1965, p. 58.

82. This was comparable to the Senate's changing of the month called *Quintilis* to *Julius* (now July) in the 40s B.C. to appease then dictator Julius Caesar.

83. Quoted in Suetonius, *Augustus* 28, in *Twelve Caesars*, p. 69.

84. Suetonius, *Augustus* 28, *Twelve Caesars*, p. 69.

85. For excellent discussions of Augustus's military reforms and their later consequences, see the brief but masterful overview in

Jones, *Augustus*, pp. 110–16; and the much more detailed analyses in Michael Grant, *The Army of the Caesars*. New York: M. Evans, 1974, pp. 36–129; Keppie, *The Making of the Roman Army*, pp. 132–90; and Chester G. Starr, *The Influence of Sea Power on Ancient History*. New York: Oxford University Press, 1989, pp. 67–81.

86. Rowell, *Rome in the Augustan Age*, p. 231.

Chapter 7: Nero: Egotist and Enemy of the People

87. In the so-called Julio-Claudian family tree, Augustus and his second wife, Scribonia, produced a daughter, Julia, who married Augustus's friend and adviser Marcus Agrippa. Julia and Agrippa had five children, including Agrippina the Elder, mother of Caligula, the third emperor; Agrippina the Elder was also mother to Agrippina the Younger, Nero's mother. Meanwhile, Livia, Augustus's third wife, had two sons from a previous marriage: Tiberius, Augustus's successor and therefore the second emperor; and Drusus the Elder; Drusus married the triumvir Mark Antony's daughter Antonia, who gave birth to Claudius, who in turn adopted Nero as his own son.

88. When Claudius adopted him, the boy's name was changed from Lucius Domitius Ahenobarbus to Nero Claudius Caesar Drusus Germanicus; for short, everyone called him Nero, the name by which he is known to posterity.

89. Suetonius, *Life of Nero* 10, in *Twelve Caesars*, p. 218.

90. Seneca, *On Mercy* 1.2–4, in *Moral Essays*. 3 vols. Translated by John W. Basore. Cambridge, MA: Harvard University Press, 1963, pp. 357–59.

91. Anthony A. Barrett, *Agrippina: Sex, Power, and Politics in the Early Empire*. New Haven, CT: Yale University Press, 1996, p. 156.

92. Suetonius, *Nero* 26, in *Twelve Caesars*, p. 227.

93. Tacitus, *Annals* 15.61, in *Tacitus: The Annals of Imperial Rome*. Translated by Michael Grant. New York: Penguin Books, 1989, p. 375.

94. Plutarch, *Life of Galba* 17.4, in *Lives of the Noble Grecians and Romans*. Translated by John Dryden. New York: Random House, 1932, p. 1,279.

95. After beginning his career working for Nero's father, Tigellinus was banished in 39 for having an affair with Nero's mother, Agrippina; later, Tigellinus was allowed to return to Rome,

where he became a horse trainer and met and became the friend of Nero. Over time, Nero promoted him to increasingly more prestigious posts.

96. Suetonius, *Nero* 21, in *Twelve Caesars*, p. 223.

97. Suetonius, *Nero* 20, in *Twelve Caesars*, p. 222.

98. Suetonius, *Nero* 23, in *Twelve Caesars*, p. 225. For a detailed discussion of Nero's attitudes toward the arts and culture, as well as his own several private and public performances, see Miriam T. Griffin, *Nero: The End of a Dynasty*. New Haven, CT: Yale University Press, 1984, pp. 119–63.

99. Tacitus, *Annals* 15.38–41, in Grant translation, pp. 362–63.

100. If Nero had started the fire, it stands to reason that he would have made sure that it did not damage some of his own imperial apartments, as in fact it did. Nor is there any strong evidence to support the famous rumor that he watched the inferno from a tower while reciting his own composition, *The Sack of Troy*, to the accompaniment of a harp (see Suetonius, *Nero* 38, in *Twelve Caesars*, pp. 235–36); Tacitus was probably more accurate in recording that the sight of the unexpected blaze reminded the emperor of the climactic event in his Trojan work, which he subsequently recited in his private theater (see *Annals* 15.40, in Grant translation, p. 363).

101. Suetonius, *Nero* 31, in *Twelve Caesars*, p. 229. The statue, created by the distinguished sculptor Zenodoros, was modeled after the famous Colossus of Rhodes, one of the seven wonders of the ancient world, prompting many Romans sarcastically to call it the "Colossus of Nero."

102. Suetonius, *Nero* 31, in *Twelve Caesars*, p. 229.

103. Suetonius, *Nero* 47, in *Twelve Caesars*, p. 242.

104. Suetonius, *Nero* 49, in *Twelve Caesars*, p. 243.

Chapter 8: Constantine: Soldier of Christ

105. Lactantius, *The Deaths of the Persecutors* 19.1–3, quoted in Michael Grant, *Constantine the Great: The Man and His Times*. New York: Scribner's, 1994, p. 21.

106. The Romans called them Picts because of their custom of painting their bodies (the Latin word *pictor* means "painter"); they began fighting the Romans, who then controlled the southern two-thirds of Britain, in about 296, and several later Roman rulers, including Constantine's son, Constans, battled them.

107. Eusebius, *Life of Constantine*, quoted in Stewart Perowne, *Caesars and Saints: The Rise of the Christian State, A.D. 180–313*. 1962. Reprinted, New York: Barnes and Noble, 1992, p. 175.

108. Most modern scholars agree with A. H. M. Jones's assessment that if Constantine did in fact see something in the sky, it was probably a solar halo, caused by the fall of "ice crystals across the rays of the sun. It usually takes the form of mock suns or of rings of light surrounding the sun, but a cross of light with the sun in its center has been on several occasions scientifically observed. The display may well have been brief . . . but to Constantine's overwrought imagination it was deeply significant" (*Constantine and the Conversion of Europe*. Toronto: University of Toronto Press, 1978, pp. 85–86). According to this view, the words "Conquer by This" and the subsequent dream were added later by Eusebius to strengthen the connection between Christ and Constantine and thereby to empower the faith.

109. In an attempt to divert suspicion from himself, Nero unjustly blamed them for starting the great fire of A.D. 64.

110. Contrary to popular belief, they did not issue the edict jointly while in Milan. During the conference, news came that Maximin had invaded some of Licinius's eastern lands; Licinius hurried to the scene, defeated his rival, and then issued the decree from Nicomedia on behalf of himself and Constantine.

111. Edict of Milan, in Eusebius, *Ecclesiastical History*. 2 vols. Translated by Roy J. Deferrari. Washington, DC: Catholic University of America Press, 1955, vol. 1, p. 269.

112. Eusebius, *Life of Constantine*, quoted in Chris Scarre, *Chronicle of the Roman Emperors*. New York: Thames and Hudson, 1995, p. 216.

113. Gibbon, *Decline and Fall*, vol. 1, p. 644. For a darker, less flattering analysis of Constantine's character, see Jones, *Constantine and the Conversion of Europe*, pp. 201–202.

114. Grant, *Constantine the Great*, pp. 190–91.

115. By now he was a committed Christian and the fact that he received this sacrament so late in life does not mean that he still harbored doubts about the faith. At the time, Averil Cameron points out, "baptism was taken very seriously and it was common to defer it as late as possible so that there was less chance of committing mortal sin subsequently" (*Later Roman Empire*, p. 59).

Chapter 9: Justinian: Preserver of Rome's Legacy

116. Grant, *History of Rome*, p. 469.

117. Robert Browning, *Justinian and Theodora*. New York: Praeger, 1971, pp. 63–64. For a more thorough discussion, see Alan Cameron, *Circus Factions: Blues and Greens at Rome and Byzantium*. Oxford: Clarendon Press, 1976.

118. Procopius, *Anecdota (Secret History)* 7.2, 25–28, in *Works*. 7 vols. Translated by H. B. Dewing. Cambridge, MA: Harvard University Press, 1961, vol. 6, pp. 77–79, 85.

119. Will Durant, *The Age of Faith*. New York: Simon and Schuster, 1950, p. 106.

120. Procopius, *Anecdota* 9.14, in *Works*, vol. 6, p. 107.

121. Procopius, *Anecdota* 15.11–12, in *Works*, vol. 6, p. 179. Note that, out of fear of Justinian and Theodora, Procopius praised both of them in his other works, written while all three were alive; the more critical *Secret History* was not published until after they were all dead. For more details about Procopius and his writings, see the introduction to the Dewing translation (note 118) and also the introductions to Averil Cameron's translation of selected passages (*Procopius*. New York: Washington Square Press, 1967) and G. A. Williamson's translation of the *Secret History* (London: Penguin Books, 1966).

122. Procopius, *Buildings* 1.1.23–24, 27, in *Works*, vol. 7, pp. 11–13.

123. Quoted in Browning, *Justinian and Theodora*, p. 104.

124. Durant, *Age of Faith*, p. 114.

125. Procopius, *History of the Wars* 4.3.14–15, 24–25, in *Works*, vol. 2, pp. 231–33.

126. Norwich, *Byzantium*, p. 263.

B.C.

ca. 1000
Primitive Roman villages exist on the seven low hills clustered near a bend in the Tiber River on the northern edge of the plain of Latium in western Italy.

753
Traditional date for the founding of Rome by the legendary king Romulus; archaeologists have confirmed that at least by this time the villages near the Tiber had combined into a central town called Rome.

509
The Romans expel their last king and establish the Roman Republic.

ca. 290
After aggressively expanding outward from the Latium plain for more than a century, the Romans complete their conquest of central Italy.

275–203
Life of Fabius Maximus, defender and savior of the Roman state during the Second Punic War.

265
Having subdued the Greek cities dotting southern Italy, the Romans are masters of the whole Italian "boot" with the exception of the Po Valley in the far north.

264–241
Years of the devastating First Punic War, in which Rome defeats Carthage.

218–202
Years of the Second Punic War, in which Rome, despite horrendous losses, manages to defeat Carthage again.

217
Fabius is appointed dictator to handle the crisis posed by the Carthaginian general Hannibal's invasion of Italy.

216
Hannibal delivers the Romans their worst defeat ever in the Battle of Cannae.

157–86
Life of Gaius Marius, the first Roman to demonstrate how a successful general could achieve political power through the personal allegiance of his soldiers.

167

Ptolemaic Egypt becomes a Roman vassal state, allowed to handle its own domestic affairs as long as it does Rome's bidding; having gained dominance over it and the other large Greek kingdoms of the western Mediterranean, Rome enjoys nearly total control of the Mediterranean world.

107

Marius is elected consul for the first of seven terms.

106–43

Life of Marcus Tullius Cicero, lawyer, orator, senator, and champion of Rome's traditional republican system.

102

Marius defeats the "barbarian" Teutones, who have invaded Rome's Gallic province (Narbonensis) and pose a threat to Italy; in the following year he crushes another group of intruders, the Cimbri.

100–44

Life of Julius Caesar, one of the greatest military generals of all time.

80

Cicero gains considerable notoriety in his first big case, in which he successfully defends Roscius, who has been accused of murdering his own father.

69

Caesar is elected quaestor; Cicero is elected aedile.

63

Cicero is elected consul; he helps save the government by exposing a planned coup by the disgruntled nobleman Catiline.

60

Julius Caesar, Gnaeus Pompey, and Marcus Crassus form a political partnership later referred to as the First Triumvirate and immediately begin to use their combined resources and powers to dominate the Roman government.

58–51

Caesar conquers the Gallic lands beyond Narbonensis, bringing them into the Roman realm.

49

Caesar crosses the Rubicon River, plunging the Roman world into a ruinous civil war.

44

Caesar is assassinated by a group of Roman senators; Octavian, Caesar's great-nephew and adopted son, makes a bid for state power.

43

Octavian joins with his two main rivals, military generals Mark Antony and Marcus Lepidus, in the alliance known as the Second Triumvirate; the triumvirs murder many of their opponents, including Cicero.

31

Octavian and his chief commander, Marcus Agrippa, advance their army and navy on Greece, where Antony and Cleopatra are amassing their own forces; on September 2, at Actium, in western Greece, the opposing navies meet in a great battle in which the famous lovers are disastrously defeated.

27

The Roman Senate confers on Octavian the name of Augustus, "the exalted one"; his ascendancy as absolute ruler marks the official end of the Roman Republic and beginning of the Roman Empire, which will dominate the Mediterranean world for over four centuries.

ca. 30 B.C.–A.D. 180

The approximate years of the so-called *Pax Romana*, or "Roman Peace," in which the Mediterranean world under the first several Roman emperors enjoys relative peace and unprecedented prosperity.

A.D.
14

Millions of Romans mourn the death of Augustus after his long, peaceful, just, and fruitful reign; the Senate declares that this reign thereafter be called the Augustan Age.

54–68

Reign of the emperor Nero, who earns a reputation as one of history's most notorious despots.

59

Nero murders his mother, Agrippina, who five years before had killed her husband, Claudius, the fourth emperor and Nero's adoptive father.

68

Declared an enemy of the people and abandoned by his own bodyguards, Nero commits suicide and is succeeded by Galba, a former provincial governor.

98–117

Reign of the emperor Trajan, in which the Roman Empire reaches its greatest size and power.

180

Death of the emperor Marcus Aurelius, marking the end of the *Pax Romana* and beginning of Rome's steady slide into economic and political crisis.

235–284

The Empire suffers under the strain of terrible political upheaval and civil strife, prompting later historians to call the third century Rome's "century of crisis" or "the anarchy."

284

Diocletian becomes emperor and initiates sweeping political, economic, and social reforms, in effect reconstructing the Empire under a new blueprint.

307–337
Reign of the emperor Constantine I, "the Great," who carries on the reforms begun by Diocletian.

312
Constantine defeats his rival, the usurper Maxentius, at Rome's Milvian Bridge.

313
Constantine and his eastern colleague, Licinius, issue the so-called Edict of Milan, granting religious toleration to the formerly hated and persecuted Christians.

330
Constantine founds the city of Constantinople, on the Bosporus, making it the capital of the eastern section of the Empire.

370
The Huns, a savage nomadic people from central Asia, sweep into eastern Europe, pushing the Goths and other "barbarian" peoples into the northern Roman provinces.

410
The Visigoths, led by Alaric, sack Rome.

476
The German-born general Odoacer deposes the young emperor, Romulus Augustulus; later historians came to see this as the "fall" of Rome, although Roman life went on more or less as usual for some time under Odoacer and other barbarian rulers.

527–565
Reign of the eastern Roman emperor Justinian, who attempts to regain the lost Roman western provinces and orders the codification of all existing Roman laws.

529
A group of scholars commissioned by Justinian introduces the *Justinian Code*, an edited compilation of centuries of Roman laws and imperial edicts; in 533, the commission publishes the *Digest*, an edited collection of jurists' interpretations of these laws.

535
Justinian's capable general Belisarius begins the reconquest of Italy, then controlled by the Ostrogoths; after twenty years, the operation is complete, but Italy is devastated and impoverished and eastern Rome fails to revitalize it; over time, the east loses control of Italy and the other former Roman territories in the west.

1453
Eastern Rome, in the form of the Byzantine Empire, falls to the Ottoman Turks.

FOR FURTHER READING

Isaac Asimov, *The Roman Empire*. Boston: Houghton Mifflin, 1967. An excellent overview of the main events of the Empire; so precise and clearly written that even very basic readers will benefit.

Lionel Casson, *Daily Life in Ancient Rome*. New York: American Heritage, 1975. A well-written presentation by a highly respected scholar of how the Romans lived: their homes, streets, entertainments, eating habits, theaters, religion, slaves, marriage customs, tombstone epitaphs, and more.

Peter Connolly, *Greece and Rome at War*. London: Macdonald, 1981. A highly informative and useful volume by one of the finest historians of ancient military affairs. Connolly, whose stunning paintings adorn this and his other books, is also the foremost modern illustrator of the ancient world. Highly recommended.

Anthony Marks and Graham Tingay, *The Romans*. London: Usborne, 1990. An excellent summary of the main aspects of Roman history, life, and arts, supported by hundreds of beautiful and accurate drawings reconstructing Roman times. Aimed at basic readers but highly recommended for anyone interested in Roman civilization.

Don Nardo, *The Roman Republic*, *The Roman Empire*, and *Cleopatra*. All San Diego: Lucent Books, 1994; *Julius Caesar*, *The Age of Augustus*, *Caesar's Conquest of Gaul*, *The Punic Wars*, and *Life in Ancient Rome*. All San Diego: Lucent Books, 1996; *Greek and Roman Mythology*, and *The Collapse of the Roman Republic*. All San Diego: Lucent Books, 1997; *The Decline and Fall of the Roman Empire* and *Life of a Roman Slave*. Both San Diego: Lucent Books, 1998. These comprehensive but easy-to-read overviews of various aspects of Roman civilization provide a broader context for understanding the leaders, trends, ideas, themes, and events of Roman history.

Jonathan Rutland, *See Inside a Roman Town*. New York: Barnes and Noble, 1986. A very attractively illustrated introduction to major concepts of Roman civilization for basic readers.

Nick Sekunda, *Roman Army, 200–104 B.C.* London: Osprey, 1996. This nicely illustrated volume by a highly respected scholar goes into great detail about Roman army personnel, uniforms, weapons, and tactics in the transitional period of the second century B.C., including the major changes made by Marius in 107–104 B.C. A must for military buffs.

Judith Simpson, *Ancient Rome*. New York: Time-Life Books, 1997. One of the latest entries in Time-Life's library of picture books about the ancient world, this one is beautifully illustrated with attractive and appropriate photographs and paintings. The general but well-written text is aimed at intermediate readers.

Chester G. Starr, *The Ancient Romans*. New York: Oxford University Press, 1971. A clearly written survey of Roman history, featuring several interesting sidebars on such subjects as the Etruscans, Roman law, and the Roman army. Also contains many primary source quotes by Roman and Greek writers. For intermediate and advanced readers.

Terence Wise, *Armies of the Carthaginian Wars, 265-146 B.C.* London: Osprey, 1996. Another handsome and useful book in Osprey's series on ancient warfare, this volume concentrates on the Roman military during the epic Punic Wars, in which Fabius, "the Delayer," played a pivotal role.

MAJOR WORKS CONSULTED

Ancient Sources

Paul J. Alexander, ed., *The Ancient World: To 300 A.D.* New York: Macmillan, 1963. A fine selection of Greek and Roman writings, including excerpts from works by Livy, Polybius, Appian, Cicero, Suetonius, and others. Also contains the *Res gestae*, the short but important work written by Augustus (Octavian).

Appian, *Roman History*. Translated by Horace White. Cambridge, MA: Harvard University Press, 1964. Appian, a second-century A.D. Romanized Greek scholar, wrote a history of Rome from about 135 to 35 B.C. that includes information on the doings of Marius, Caesar, and Cicero, as well as Octavian's (Augustus's) early career. Books 13–17 of the work are commonly referred to or published separately as the *Civil Wars*, covering in some detail the strife of the first century B.C. and fall of the Republic. A very fine recent edition, from which I quote, is *Appian: The Civil Wars*. Translated by John Carter. New York: Penguin Books, 1996.

Julius Caesar, *Commentary on the Gallic War* and *Commentary on the Civil Wars*, published as *War Commentaries of Caesar*. Translated by Rex Warner. New York: New American Library, 1960. Caesar, as gifted a writer as he was a general and politician, left behind these fabulously detailed accounts of his personal battlefield and campaign experiences, affording us a fascinating glimpse into the mind of one of the greatest military leaders who ever lived.

Cicero, *Letters to Atticus*. 3 vols. Translated by E. O. Winstedt. Cambridge, MA: Harvard University Press, 1961; *Letters to His Friends*. 3 vols. Translated by W. Glynn Williams. Cambridge, MA: Harvard University Press, 1965; *De Officiis*. Translated by Walter Miller. Cambridge, MA: Harvard University Press, 1961; *Selected Political Speeches of Cicero*. Translated by Michael Grant. Baltimore: Penguin Books, 1979; *The Basic Works of Cicero*. Edited by Moses Hadas. New York: Random House, 1951; *Cicero: The Nature of the Gods*. Translated by Horace C. P. McGregor. New York: Penguin Books, 1972; *Cicero: Selected Works*. Translated by Michael Grant. New York: Penguin Books, 1971; and *Cicero: Murder Trials*. Translated by Michael Grant. New York: Penguin Books, 1990. Cicero's letters, speeches, and essays contain a wealth of information about first-century B.C. Roman leaders (including himself, Marius, Caesar, and Octavian), the major political and social events of the era, and the attitudes and viewpoints of the Roman upper classes of his day.

Dio Cassius, *Roman History: The Reign of Augustus*. Translated by Ian Scott-Kilvert. New York: Penguin Books, 1987. An excellent translation of Dio's important work about the events of Augustus Caesar's (Octavian's) rise to power and reign as the first Roman emperor.

Eusebius, *Ecclesiastical History*. 2 vols. Translated by Roy J. Deferrari. Washington, DC: Catholic University of America Press, 1955. This chronicle of the struggles of the early Christians by Eusebius, one of the most important of the early church fathers (who also wrote a biography of the emperor Constantine), contains descriptions of several Christian persecutions, as well as a transcription of the famous Edict of Milan, coauthored by Constantine.

G. B. Harrison, ed., *Julius Caesar in Shakespeare, Shaw, and the Ancients*. New York: Harcourt, Brace, and World, 1960. This extremely useful volume is a grab bag of works by and about Caesar, including Shakespeare's *Julius Caesar,* Shaw's *Caesar and Cleopatra*, Suetonius's and Plutarch's biographies of Caesar, and excerpts from Cicero's letters and Caesar's own Gallic commentaries. Highly recommended.

Lactantius, *The Deaths of the Persecutors*, in *Lactantius: Minor Works*. Translated by Sister Mary Francis McDonald. Washington, DC: Catholic University of America Press, 1965. This work by the early Christian apologist Lactantius, whose formal name was Lucius Caelius Firmianus, contains a vivid description of the emperor Diocletian's persecution of the Christian sect.

Naphtali Lewis and Meyer Reinhold, eds., *Roman Civilization: Sourcebook I: The Republic*, and *Roman Civilization: Sourcebook II: The Empire*. Both New York: Harper and Row, 1966. Huge, comprehensive collections of original Roman documents, from the founding of the city to its fall, including inscriptions, papyri, and government edicts, as well as formal writings by authors ranging from Livy to Cicero to St. Augustine. Both contain much useful commentary.

Livy, *The History of Rome from Its Foundation*. Books 1–5 published as *Livy: The Early History of Rome*. Translated by Aubrey de Sélincourt. New York: Penguin Books, 1971; books 21–30 published as *Livy: The War with Hannibal*. Translated by Aubrey de Sélincourt. New York: Penguin Books, 1972. Excellent translations of these parts of Livy's massive and masterful history, written during Rome's golden literary age of the late first century B.C. The first volume contains the most extensive available primary source descriptions of Romulus and the Roman foundation, and the second includes most of what is known about the career and exploits of Fabius Maximus.

Plutarch, *Lives of the Noble Grecians and Romans.* Translated by John Dryden. New York: Random House, 1932; also excerpted in *Fall of the Roman Republic: Six Lives by Plutarch.* Translated by Rex Warner. New York: Penguin Books, 1972; and *Makers of Rome: Nine Lives By Plutarch.* Translated by Ian Scott-Kilvert. New York: Penguin Books, 1965. We are indebted to Plutarch, a Greek who lived and wrote in the late first and early second centuries A.D., for his biographies of ancient Greek and Roman figures, including Romulus, Rome's founder; Fabius Maximus, who squared off against Hannibal in the Second Punic War; and various notables from the era of the collapsing Republic, including Marius, Sulla, Pompey, Caesar, Cicero, and Antony.

Polybius, *The Histories*, published as *Polybius: The Rise of the Roman Empire.* Translated by Ian Scott-Kilvert. New York: Penguin Books, 1979. This Greek historian's works are valuable for their often detailed coverage of the wars Rome fought against Carthage and the Greek kingdoms of the eastern Mediterranean during the third and second centuries B.C.

Procopius, *Works.* 7 vols. Translated by H. B. Dewing. Cambridge, MA: Harvard University Press, 1961. The works of the Byzantine historian Procopius (ca. A.D. 500–555), including the *Wars*, the *Buildings*, and the *Secret History*, are the principal primary sources of information for the reign of the eastern Roman emperor Justinian and that ruler's colorful wife, Theodora.

Sallust, *Works.* Translated by J. C. Rolfe. New York: Cambridge University Press, 1965; also *Sallust: The Jugurthine War/The Conspiracy of Catiline.* Translated by S. A. Handford. New York: Penguin Books, 1988. *The Jugurthine War*, by Sallust, one of the most honest and insightful of Roman historians, is one of the three principal ancient sources about the great general Gaius Marius (the other two being works by Plutarch and Cicero). Sallust's *The Conspiracy of* (or *War with*) *Catiline* is the most important source of information about the attempted military coup by the disgruntled nobleman Catiline, an episode that did much to shape the careers of Cicero and Caesar.

Seneca, *Moral Essays.* 3 vols. Translated by John W. Basore. Cambridge, MA: Harvard University Press, 1963. Seneca (ca. 4 B.C.– A.D. 65) was a talented, urbane, and brilliant Stoic philosopher and playwright who served as tutor and court adviser to the notorious emperor Nero. Of main interest here is Seneca's essay *On Mercy* (or *On Clemency*), addressed to Nero (see vol. 1, pp. 357–449).

Suetonius, *Lives of the Twelve Caesars*, published as *The Twelve Caesars*. Translated by Robert Graves and revised by Michael Grant. New York: Penguin Books, 1979. Suetonius's biographies of Caesar, Augustus, and Nero contain much valuable information about these monumental Roman figures, as well as tangential facts about Caesar's distinguished opponent Cicero.

Tacitus, *Annals*, published as *Tacitus: The Annals of Imperial Rome*. Translated by Michael Grant. New York: Penguin Books, 1989; and *Histories*, published as *Tacitus: The Histories*. Translated by Kenneth Wellesley. New York: Penguin Books, 1993. The works of Cornelius Tacitus (ca. A.D. 55–120), one of the greatest of all ancient historians, contain numerous references to and anecdotes about Julius Caesar, Octavian/Augustus, and Nero.

Modern Sources

E. Badian, *Roman Imperialism in the Late Republic*. Ithaca, NY: Cornell University Press, 1968. A scholarly work that examines Roman partisan politics, greed, and the drive for foreign expansion in the Republic's last two and most turbulent centuries, including the exploits of Marius and Caesar.

Robert Browning, *Justinian and Theodora*. New York: Praeger, 1971. A well-written, useful general overview of Justinian, his controversial wife, Theodora, the powerful men surrounding him (Belisarius, Narses, John of Cappadocia, and others), his expeditions to recapture Africa and Italy, and the bitter religious divisions within his empire.

Averil Cameron, *The Later Roman Empire: A.D. 284–430*. Cambridge, MA: Harvard University Press, 1993. Contains excellent general, up-to-date summaries of Diocletian's administrative and other reforms and Constantine's own reforms, including his acceptance of Christianity.

F. R. Cowell, *Cicero and the Roman Republic*. Baltimore: Penguin Books, 1967. A very detailed and insightful analysis of the late Republic, its leaders (Cicero, Caesar, and Octavian prominent among them), and the problems that led to its collapse. Very highly recommended.

Michael Crawford, *The Roman Republic*. Cambridge, MA: Harvard University Press, 1993. One of the best available overviews of the Republic, offering various insights into the nature of the political, cultural, and intellectual forces that shaped the decisions of Roman leaders, including Fabius, Marius, Caesar, Cicero, and Octavian.

Gavin de Beer, *Hannibal: Challenging Rome's Supremacy*. New York: Viking Press, 1969. A detailed scholarly account of the Second Punic War, in which Fabius Maximus, Rome's "Shield," played a crucial role.

John B. Firth, *Augustus Caesar and the Organization of the Empire of Rome*. Freeport, NY: Books for the Libraries Press, 1972. Beginning with Caesar's assassination in 44 B.C., this is a detailed, thoughtful telling of the final years of the Republic, including Octavian's rise to power during the civil wars and his ascendancy as Augustus, the first Roman emperor.

Michael Grant, *Caesar*. London: Weidenfeld and Nicolson, 1974. A fine biography by one of the most prolific of classical historians.

———, *Constantine the Great: The Man and His Times*. New York: Scribner's, 1994. A very fine study of Constantine, his achievements (Christianity, Constantinople, etc.), and his impact on the Roman Empire and later ages.

———, *History of Rome*. New York: Scribner's, 1978. Comprehensive, insightful, and well written, this is one of the best available general overviews of Roman civilization from its founding to its fall.

Miriam T. Griffin, *Nero: The End of a Dynasty*. New Haven, CT: Yale University Press, 1984. Griffin, a distinguished scholar of Somerville College, Oxford, here delivers a commendable, readable, very well documented study of one of the most colorful and reviled of Rome's leaders. Highly recommended.

A. H. M. Jones, *Constantine and the Conversion of Europe*. Toronto: University of Toronto Press, 1978. A superior general overview of Constantine's world and his influence, particularly in the area of religion, by one of the twentieth century's two or three greatest Roman scholars.

Ramsay MacMullen, *Roman Government's Response to Crisis: A.D. 235–337*. New Haven, CT: Yale University Press, 1976. A worthwhile overview of the crisis years following the end of the Severan dynasty and the reorganization of the Empire by Diocletian and Constantine.

Christian Meier, *Caesar*. Translated by David McLintock. New York: HarperCollins, 1996. This latest major biography of the great Roman general and statesman is already ranked by many critics among the two or three most comprehensive and authoritative.

Thomas N. Mitchell, *Cicero: The Senior Statesman*. New Haven, CT: Yale University Press, 1991. An informative, up-to-date study of the great politician, orator, writer, courageous champion of the disintegrating Republic, and one of the most important and influential literary figures in Western history.

ADDITIONAL WORKS CONSULTED

Lesley Adkins and Roy A. Adkins, *Handbook to Life in Ancient Rome*. New York: Facts On File, 1994.

Timothy D. Barnes, *Constantine and Eusebius*. Cambridge, MA: Harvard University Press, 1981.

Anthony A. Barrett, *Agrippina: Sex, Power, and Politics in the Early Empire*. New Haven, CT: Yale University Press, 1996.

Mary Beard and Michael Crawford, *Rome in the Late Republic: Problems and Interpretations*. London: Duckworth, 1985.

Arthur E. R. Boak, *A History of Rome to 565 A.D.* New York: Macmillan, 1943.

Ernle Bradford, *Julius Caesar: The Pursuit of Power*. New York: Morrow, 1984.

John Buchan, *Augustus*. London: Hodder and Stoughton, 1937.

Matthew Bunson, *A Dictionary of the Roman Empire*. Oxford: Oxford University Press, 1991.

Owen Chadwick, *A History of Christianity*. New York: St. Martin's Press, 1995.

Gilbert Charles-Picard, *Augustus and Nero: The Secret of Empire*. Translated by Len Ortzen. New York: Thomas Y. Crowell, 1965.

Tim Cornell and John Matthews, *Atlas of the Roman World*. New York: Facts On File, 1982.

T. J. Cornell, *The Beginnings of Rome: Italy and Rome from the Bronze Age to the Punic Wars (c.1000–264 B.C.)*. London: Routledge, 1995.

Will Durant, *The Age of Faith*. New York: Simon and Schuster, 1950.

Charles Freeman, *Egypt, Greece, and Rome: Civilizations of the Ancient Mediterranean*. Oxford: Oxford University Press, 1996.

———, *The World of the Romans*. New York: Oxford University Press, 1993.

J. F. C. Fuller, *Julius Caesar: Man, Soldier, and Tyrant*. New Brunswick, NJ: Rutgers University Press, 1965.

Matthias Gelzer, *Caesar: Politician and Statesman*. Cambridge, MA: Harvard University Press, 1968.

Edward Gibbon, *The Decline and Fall of the Roman Empire*. 3 vols. Edited by David Womersley. New York: Penguin Books, 1994.

Michael Grant, *The Army of the Caesars*. New York: M. Evans, 1974.

———, *Atlas of Classical History*. New York: Oxford University Press, 1994.

———, *The Roman Emperors*. New York: Barnes and Noble, 1997.

———, *The World of Rome*. New York: New American Library, 1960.

Sir John Hackett, ed., *Warfare in the Ancient World*. New York: Facts On File, 1989.

A. H. M. Jones, *Augustus*. New York: W. W. Norton, 1970.

———, *The Decline of the Ancient World*. London: Longman, 1966.

Solomon Katz, *The Decline of Rome and the Rise of Medieval Europe*. Ithaca, NY: Cornell University Press, 1955.

Lawrence Keppie, *The Making of the Roman Army*. New York: Barnes and Noble, 1994.

Phillip A. Kildahl, *Caius Marius*. New York: Twayne, 1968.

Ramsay MacMullen, *Constantine*. New York: Dial Press, 1969.

John J. Norwich, *Byzantium: The Early Centuries*. New York: Knopf, 1989.

Torsten Petersson, *Cicero: A Biography*. New York: Biblo and Tannen, 1963.

John C. Rolfe, *Cicero and His Influence*. New York: Cooper Square, 1963.

Michael Rostovtzeff, *Rome*. Translated by Elias J. Bickerman. London: Oxford University Press, 1960.

Henry T. Rowell, *Rome in the Augustan Age*. Norman: University of Oklahoma Press, 1962.

Chris Scarre, *Chronicle of the Roman Emperors*. New York: Thames and Hudson, 1995.

———, *Historical Atlas of Ancient Rome*. New York: Penguin Books, 1995.

Chester G. Starr, *Civilization and the Caesars: The Intellectual Revolution in the Roman Empire*. New York: Norton, 1965.

———, *A History of the Ancient World*. New York: Oxford University Press, 1991.

———, *The Influence of Sea Power on Ancient History*. New York: Oxford University Press, 1989.

Lily Ross Taylor, *Party Politics in the Age of Caesar*. Berkeley and Los Angeles: University of California Press, 1968.

L. P. Wilkinson, *The Roman Experience*. Lanham, MD: University Press of America, 1974.

INDEX

PICTURE CREDITS

ABOUT THE AUTHOR

Classical historian and award-winning writer Don Nardo has published more than twenty books about the ancient Greek and Roman world. These include general histories, such as *The Roman Empire, The Persian Empire,* and *Philip and Alexander: The Unification of Greece*; war chronicles, such as *The Punic Wars* and *The Battle of Marathon*; cultural studies such as *Life in Ancient Greece, Greek and Roman Theater, The Age of Augustus,* and *The Trial of Socrates*; and literary companions to the works of Homer and Sophocles. Mr. Nardo also writes screenplays and teleplays and composes music. He lives with his lovely wife, Christine, and dog, Bud, on Cape Cod, Massachusetts.